GREEK ETHICAL THOUGHT
FROM HOMER TO THE STOICS

GREEK
ETHICAL THOUGHT

FROM HOMER TO THE STOICS

BY

HILDA D. OAKELEY

BOOKS FOR LIBRARIES PRESS
FREEPORT, NEW YORK

First Published 1925
Reprinted 1971

INTERNATIONAL STANDARD BOOK NUMBER:
0-8369-5751-2

LIBRARY OF CONGRESS CATALOG CARD NUMBER:
76-152999

PRINTED IN THE UNITED STATES OF AMERICA

To

J. E. V. AND M. H. V

INTRODUCTION

WE are accustomed to think of the ethical ideas of the Greeks as determined by a standpoint which can be definitely contrasted with the modern. It is thought to involve a different attitude to life and death, the questions of man's relation to the world, the meaning of duty, if not the meaning of good. The Greek ideal has, for instance, been contrasted as "affirmation of the world," with the Christian, as "denial of the world." Or, if it is recognised that the Greek views in regard to a worthy life, the most fitting way of meeting alike the best gifts, and the "slings and arrows" of fortune, had much in common with our own, it is nevertheless felt probably by most of us, that there is a subtle, all-pervasive contrast due perhaps to the difference of the medium, the environment of thought, knowledge, experience in which these views prevailed. A certain circle or ideas, as it may be said, in connection with practical life, must arise whenever a people reaches that stage of culture at which man desires in some sense, in some measure, to shape himself his history. These ideas emerge when individuals no longer feel themselves fast bound to some one mode of existence whose form is rigidly determined by tradition and custom, but seem capable of freely reflecting upon their life and directing it to ends which they desire. But the Greek ways of interpreting the chief problems which beset human existence, and those conceptions which return from age to age, as to what gives it value, and how this value may be secured or increased, belonged to a spiritual atmosphere very unlike that of the modern world. This unlikeness, it may be assumed, would be due in general to their different historic situation, and in particular to the different world-view which belonged to it, the different imagination concerning what lies behind and beyond the human scene.

There is certainly much truth in such contrasts. We cannot re-create the spirit which produced the Greek treatment of life. Can we indeed re-create even the spirit of a century ago, when the last representatives of an age that has passed away are no longer in our midst enabling us by living sympathy to place ourselves at their point of view? Nevertheless in the case of the Greeks the incomparable power with which they expressed their thought about life has provided an atmosphere of great art through which their genius can as it were invite all who seek to know something of their spirit to " come and see." In reading their words and steeping ourselves in their literature and philosophy, we seem at least to come more nearly to a vision of their practical outlook than is possible in the case of any other race or age of past time.

In spite of the sense of distance, the more we study the Greek writings on the central questions of practice, the more deeply we are impressed by the range of moral experience covered by the Greek mind. If we turn first to the literature which gives expression to ideas belonging to the earlier stage of moral history, we find those sub-rational beliefs which dominate conduct by a kind of iron necessity in ages before the individual can form, with some measure of independence, his own thoughts upon his actions, and amongst them beliefs apparently shared by primitive peoples generally. As Professor Gilbert Murray says, " There is hardly any horror of primitive superstition of which we cannot find some distant traces in our Greek record." Pursuing our way from the Epic Poets through the Tragic drama to the philosophers, we seem to pass through the whole scale of ideas revolving round the central thought of conduct as a thing commanded. We begin with man as under compulsion of destiny driving him to complete the dread unfinished deed from generation to generation. We rise to the thought of man as attaining the vision of the Good, and thereafter necessarily obedient to that vision. Or we may prefer to describe the passage as one from bondage to the idea of a blind force to which man is enslaved, to service to the idea which gives freedom. As Stoicism in the later stage of Greek history completed the thought—freedom lies in the acceptance of that universal law which proceeds from the Mind to which our own is akin.

The Greek genius as expressed in its greatest poets drew out of the crude and harsh conceptions belonging to the barbarous stage of human history all the moral meaning of which they were capable. Here in the development of the Greek moral spirit, we are not scanning features of humanity wholly strange to us, but beholding as it were in a glass the outlines of the history of the universal human spirit. The tragedy of humanity is symbolised in the tragedy of minds in dawning rationalism and individualism, wrestling with conceptions of what man is bound to do deeply rooted in the sub-rational nature. The problem whether the will is still the essential self, though, not led by clear vision, it cannot be disentangled from blinding circumstance, is presented by Sophocles through the legend of Oedipus as a tremendous moral parable. Some of the personalities of Euripides, nearer than those of Sophocles to the men and women we know, appear as though constrained by their situation in life to behave in accordance with an outworn tradition against which they are already rebellious, though they dream at intervals the old dream of their race. It is because the Greek spirit, at its height, could pass so swiftly from tribal to universal, illuminating the first confused notions of the being " that

was and was not man " with the light of humanism, that on
the basis of the tribal ethic, eternally human experiences,
the purifying effects of suffering, the necessary passage of
justice from retribution to equity and mercy, are presented
with truth and undying beauty and the religion of sacrifice
is almost reached. Never has this spirit been more perfectly
expressed outside the New Testament than in the *Prometheus*
of Aeschylus.

When we dwell upon the character of the Greek interpretation of life thus suggested, in which there grow out
of the lowly roots of man's first dark guesses about rules of
action which raise him above the animal, the finest flowers
of the idealism of duty, we might expect to find in this
people a complete philosophy of conduct from this point
of view. It has often been pointed out that the philosophy
of duty in its greatest modern exponent Immanuel Kant
requires for its explanation the previous history of Christian
thought. The intense expression in the *Ethics* of Kant of
the dualism of the practical consciousness, the overwhelming
force of moral responsibility, these it is thought become
possible only through the Christian ideas of the crisis of the
world in the struggle between good and evil, the momentous
importance of individual destiny. Whilst recognising the
truth of this estimate, we must also allow that Greek culture
was not without powerful witnesses to conceptions of the
practical life which belong to the range of ideas of which
duty is the centre. They are prepared for in the sombre
representation of the accumulated force of the past bearing
upon the present, of which the drama presents sublime and
terrible illustrations. They have their earlier form in the
view of practice as determined by consciousness of a law to
be obeyed, action to be performed not because it will have
any good outcome, but because it is required by a greater
will with intent not fully known to the man who acts. The

situation of the individuals as conforming to a destiny in which
they seem at times to be pawns is the more striking because
of the towering personalities of such chief agents as the
Clytemnestra of Aeschylus, or the intellectual power, in
virtue of which they are never mere unreasoning tools of
superhuman powers, as in the Oedipus of Sophocles. Far
indeed is the treatment of the idea of destiny in the drama
from the earlier conception in epic poetry of the force which
overshadows human life. The Homeric Fate belongs essentially to the spirit we call Paganism. It is attached to the
picture of the joy and pathos of life as lived by the highest
of animal beings, " looking before and after," but not looking very far or deeply. Awake to all the splendour and
enchantment of conscious existence with a vividness surpassing anything that can be experienced in an older civilisation, the Homeric men are glad to silence the questions that
might sickly it with thought by the reflection that man will
never escape Fate. Nevertheless, since the decrees of destiny
are quite incalculable, there is no such compulsion as is felt
by the personages of the drama to co-operate in their execution, and the Homeric man is so far care-free in respect to
the divine intent. The thought of an inescapable destiny
wholly non-human in its sources seems to lend to Homeric
life rather an added brilliance, when we contrast it with the
awful burden of the individual of Aeschylus or Sophocles,
marked out to achieve in his own acts, consciously if unwillingly, the destined end. Human life must be transient,
since its glory would depart, if men clave to it and feared to
die, or if they outlived long their time of strength. Not in
Homer's treatment of the idea of destiny, but in that of the
drama do we recognise, if we penetrate behind the richly
adorned cloak of the Greek racial imagination, a kinship to
the moral results of the religion of duty.

Paganism fully rationalised has—though Aristotle sometimes

takes us beyond it—its philosophic expression in Aristotle's *Ethics*. Here is presented the perfection of a life for man fully conscious of the reason of its essential value beyond the value of mere life. It is reason which shows him that he can create a new thing in the world, the rational society which makes life good. Here is still the spirit of Paganism scarcely troubled by the thought of the Infinite, so long at least as Aristotle remains at the practical standpoint. It is in the ethical philosophy of Plato that the movement of the Greek genius on that pathway revealed to us in the drama is not forgotten. In its greatest thinker, the whole history of the Greek spirit seems to culminate, and the fruits of its travail over the burden and mystery of man's short and narrow life are behind his speculations on " all time and all existence." The contrast between the practical philosophies of Plato and Aristotle represents, all the more impressively because they are both so essentially Greek, that conflict within the Greek moral ideal which is the conflict of ethical thought universally. Aristotle was the first philosopher who wrote a treatise on Ethics as a subject by itself, and as we have seen, it was not because Greek thought had not pondered deeply on the problems associated with the sense of moral obligation, the place of suffering and sacrifice, the consciousness of guilt, that, on the whole and in his general attitude, he passed them by. It was rather because, as soon as the standpoint of rational reflection upon life is adopted by a thinker who is primarily a logician and fundamentally scientific in his interest, he almost necessarily assumes that he has something to deal with which can be intellectually understood, through and through. Seeking the principles of conduct, as he has sought the laws of nature, he abstracts from the course of human action that wholly intelligible relation of conscious purpose to end, or goal, which is in a special sense the prerogative of man. Greek ethical theory and method, taking a systematic form in Aristotle, expresses the striving of the people towards that light which reason can give, in the knowledge of the world. It is a recoil from all that cannot be lucidly formulated in the only rational formulation they could conceive. Life is no longer to be a tale told by an idiot. For the idiot we must substitute the wise man. Intellect fully aroused, and dazzled by its own achievements in other spheres, which seem to have boundless promise, will surely know how to silence and curb even the sound and fury of passionate life. The chaotic world of desire and emotion can be dominated, and the principles of harmony and measure supreme in art make of human existence a perfect work, an energy in accordance with reason and all excellence. What is the good? How attained? Is there an absolutely satisfying end of that striving which seems to be the universal character even of animal existence? For this character has no meaning or intelligibility unless the striving leads to a goal through which the innumerable forms it takes can be unified. To the question "Who will show us any good?" the great moralist seems to reply that the pathway to the good in human life is clearly to be found by a careful examination of human nature and its distinctive features. This type of thought has, to use a modern expression, an "inner-worldly" character. It treats ethics as a study in which, in the phrase of Cicero's interpretation of Socrates, philosophy is "brought down from heaven to earth." The most rationalistic thinker of Greece asks his countrymen to turn their gaze away from the infinity encompassing man's life, and so far at least as they mean to be practical, to see themselves, not in the light of eternity, but in the light of the City state. For it is this creation of reason and culture, in the midst of a world for the most part still barbaric, which artistically handled will give them scope for the best life. It is for them to make of it all that it can be, as an instrument

for development of the highest human potentialities, with
friendship as the ideal type of the social bond, the only
atmosphere in which complete self-realisation is possible.
Here is the good for man. It is evident that if with Plato
he strains after some eternal unchanging good in itself, he
will miss the mark in life. For even Plato admitted that
those who fix their gaze upon such a transcendent ideal and
desire to live in its too dazzling light, have some difficulty
in finding their way about the actual world. Thus Aristotle's
discerning knowledge of the world persuades the spirit of a
noble common sense in the practical man. But he fails to
allow for the paradox of the practical experience, its need to
orient itself to the eternal just because it is finite, its demand
for a good not found in the world of "appearance." The
moral consciousness of humanity, if it seek its exemplar in
Greek philosophical ethics, does not find all that it seeks in
Aristotle. It requires also the prophetic outlook which
Plato combines with the scientific in his treatment of the
practical life.

We may now turn to a further consideration of certain
principles which pervade Greek thought upon ethics generally, though they enter in different ways into the reflection
of the philosophers, according to the main differences of
standpoint which have been indicated. Amongst the most
characteristic of these, and probably the best known, is the
idea of the good life as a harmony in which all the different
powers co-operate so that the practical experience is a unity
though filled with the activities that appeal to all parts of
man's nature. The sources of reflection on this idea, which
seems native to the Greek genius, lie far back in the mental
history of the race. Thoughts of the early philosophers,
originally perhaps borrowed unconsciously from social experience, suggest that the order of nature itself requires that
measure and restraint shall be observed in the relation of the

different forces to each other. According to Anaximander, the elements, having encroached upon each other's spheres, " render compensation to one another for their injustice." Heraclitus, who proclaims the harmony of opposites as the secret of the world, declares that " the sun shall not exceed his measures." Above all, the Pythagoreans conceived the law of harmony as pervading all spheres of nature and life, from the starry heavens to the human soul, which they are said to have defined as itself a harmony, whilst in music and medicine the same principle prevailed. In Pythagoreanism was developed the peculiar relation between the principle of reason and order, and that of the " finite " as form and definiteness impressed upon the indefinite and chaotic in all spheres. This was associated with their mathematical philosophy, for which number was the nature of things, and connected with a dualistic view, for good was everywhere " finite "—that is, it exhibited order and form; whilst evil was " infinite," or formless, disordered, manifold. The Pythagorean way of thinking seems to have had much influence on Plato, and in a lesser degree on Aristotle in connection with his definition of " virtue as a mean." But the general conception that all things good express a quality of harmony, and proportion, a due balance of all their elements, is recognised by students of the varied manifestations of Greek genius to be a factor inseparable from its outlook and activity. Prior to philosophic ethics it dictates some of those leading judgments or categories by which it was attempted to understand the course of events in the lives of individuals and peoples, otherwise baffling to thought. The great extremes of power and fortune, immoderate ambition, overweening pride, destroy the right balance and measure of life, and will bring down divine chastisement, inevitable fate. So Herodotus puts into the mouth of the wise man Solon the condemnation of " Hybris " or the self-exaltation which aspires to power beyond what is due for man, and the description of a happy life in the moderate fortunes of the good son, who tends his flock in simplicity and performs the sacred family duties. And the greatest illustration of Hybris in the Persian wars is the theme of Aeschylus and Herodotus as the tragedy of Xerxes' fall.

In Thucydides also we may trace the presence of the notion of Hybris in the vivid presentation of the hatred felt by the Greek states for the Athenian Empire and Athens as the tyrant city which had arisen in Greece.

In Plato's pitiless analysis of the moral dangers of power (which seems to occupy in his ethics the place given to riches in the New Testament), the destiny of the tyrant with a tyrant's nature follows not from an external law of fate, but from the inner necessity of character. But his picture of the misery of the tyrannic soul, slave to a tyrannous passion, takes something of its colour from the old idea of Hybris. The principle of harmony receives its most perfect application to the moral life in the ethics of Plato, because for him, as apparently for the Pythagoreans, it was a universal principle, and the good in human life is an image, reflection, or counterpart in the microcosm, of the good in the all, or the Cosmos. On the whole, though (as will be noticed), there is another and very different point of view in Platonism— the idea of harmony is a principle of explanation in a great part of his moral teaching. It appears as constituting the virtue which is the necessary ground of cohesion and unity in the Republic, regarded as justice, or the principle that each individual and each class shall do its own true task, the work whose performance is its proper function and life. Again this virtue is temperance, complementary to justice and enabling all to recognise their due relation to each other. On the external side the influences of harmony are to enter the souls of the people in youth, since their early lives will be spent in the midst of fair sights and fair sounds. Plato is a true Greek in his belief in beauty as an ally to morality; whilst as a philosophic idealist, he sees the ground of this practical truth in the real nature of the Good, which is also Beauty. In this respect his doctrine of the Universe involves the unity of all value, in one source of good, beauty, and truth; and human life, so far as good, presents in some measure a reflection of this unity. The eternal good of the Republic is conceived in the *Symposium* as eternal Beauty, and the progress of the individual in goodness, as an increasing capacity to rise from the visible to the invisible beauty, from loveliness in earthly objects to beauty of deeds and thoughts, until he can contemplate the ideal Beauty. The dialogue *Philebus* describes and analyses the elements of the good as man can find it in life, and arguing that they can only proceed from the cosmic good, defines the nature of this. Its character is threefold, Beauty, Symmetry and Truth.

A whole phase in the history of the Greek mind thus enters into the characterisation of the good life by the philosophers in the light of the principles of harmony and measure. It is not merely that good and beauty are so nearly akin, but that beauty everywhere is manifested as form, and the order-giving law in thought and the world must therefore be supreme also in human conduct, if this is to strive after perfection. In all its fulness this conception is only found in Plato, and his treatment of the law of measure in life must therefore be present to us, if we are to understand the more restricted and common-sense use of the notion in Aristotle. To the Greeks who knew the lineage of Aristotle's doctrine of "the mean," and from what springs it drew its quality, it could not have been confused with any merely quantitative estimate of the difference between virtue and vice as by some modern thinkers. They would feel that the ancient saying, "Never too much," did not carry with it permission for an

B

easy abatement of moral effort, but the setting up of a very difficult ideal of the exactly due path in action, deviating neither to the right nor to the left, determined by no calculating balance of goods, but the unrestricted enthusiasm for the best. " Evil is many, but good is only one," a Pythagorean dictum, not far from the maxim that " Strait is the gate and narrow the way." At least this is how we must understand the Platonic significance of the principle of measure in the practical life, associated as it is both with a profounder consciousness than is expressed elsewhere in Greek philosophy, of the elements in human nature which war against order, and self-restraint, and also with a higher ideal of duty. And though shorn in Aristotle of its far-reaching significance, the doctrine of the mean is clearly presented as involving the highest moral effort, reaching even, at times, to extreme self-sacrifice. " From the point of view of the best and the ideal, virtue is an extreme. It is a mean only in so far as we are logically defining it."

Aristotle is perhaps liable to be carried away by the satisfaction he finds in acute analysis and classification of the subject-matter he is dealing with, when he makes the most of the fact he has noticed that the principle of measure may be literally illustrated in practice, if we conceive every virtuous action as contrasting with the wrong in two opposing directions. But the opposition is not of extremes within the proper sphere of ethics, one moral, one immoral, with a mean which is moderation in virtue. The extremes are in the raw material of ethics, passions, emotions, desires, in regard to which the good man always has that proportion which is necessary for virtue. What the proportion is is not a question for calculation—as for instance how much fearlessness is the due amount for courage so that it shall neither pass into rashness nor fall into timidity. It is a question to be answered on quite other grounds in the light of what is " noble." It seems if we consider together all the passages in which Aris.otle refers to the criterion of virtue as the " noble " or " beautiful," that this may be taken to answer on the whole to what we mean by the moral ideal, though it must be noticed that in Aristotle's suggestion the ideal carries with it a reference to the world's praise not admissible for the modern moralist nor certainly for Plato. It is the full consciousness of the ideal which enables the virtuous man to hit the centre or the perfect mean, giving, for instance, where it is a question of liberality, the due amount to the right person at the proper time, for the right reason, and in the right way. And should he hesitate in connection with any of these details, he must refer to the standard of practical reason, and ask how the man of practical insight would act.

With this introduction of the criterion of practical reason or wisdom of life we come upon another leading principle in the structure of Greek ethics, which again in its significance for he Greeks belongs to the essential poise of their spirit and the history of their thought. It has already been noticed that in the conception of the practical life as a material in our hands as it were, to be artistically and rationally shaped and directed to the attainment of the highest good for man, Aristotle presents what seems to be the natural view of reason when with full self-consciousness it turns to the problem of the organisation of human life. But in regard to the interpretation of the place of thought in life and the doctrine of the practically wise man, there is something peculiar to the Greek point of view. It may be said that one source at least of the profound pathos of the literature of life from Homer to Euripides lies in the sense of the comparative impotence of that power of intellect which seemed to this gifted people so divine a possession, to control or even modify human destiny, to save man from destroying with his own hands the treasures of experience he most prized. The endowment of

the strong mind and penetrating thought is valued as in
Homer's Odysseus, sometimes more than courage, the all-
important virtue in the long ages of growth behind the
cultured community. May one not say that the place of the
Prophet in the life of Israel is taken by the supremely wise
man in Greek ethic? It was the deep thought of Prometheus
which, turning to the misery of primitive man, provided him
with Fire and the indispensable conditions of the arts raising
him above the beasts. The tragedy of Oedipus as Sophocles
conceives it, lies especially in the ignorance, in the most vital
matters, of the man whose intellect had once made him the
saviour of his people, as his blindness to the truth now brings
down upon them a curse.

Turning to the actual figures of Greek history, it is
fitting that the greatest personality of this people should
have combined in himself, in character, life, and way of
thought, the ideal of the wise man equally inspiring as a
stimulus for the philosophy of knowledge and of life, and
that his martyrdom should have been a martyrdom for truth
in both fields. In Socrates the Delphic precept, "Know
thyself," became a moving force for the construction of
Greek philosophical ethics; self-knowledge must be the
basis of practical life and perhaps also, as appears when this
principle has set to work in the mind of Plato, for knowledge of the universe. The vexed question of the relation of
Plato to Socrates is, I think, best grappled with, if we bear
in mind that it was one of the greatest moral personalities
of history whose power had subdued to its outlook upon life
the great philosophic genius at his most impressionable period
of intellectual growth. This aspect at least of the relation of
the two men does much to explain the dominant ethical
note of Plato's philosophy, and the fact that his greatest
speculative flights always have a bearing upon practice, and
the right way of life. The mighty form of Socrates pervades

almost the whole work of Plato's genius. The monument of
Socrates is that he is the spirit of philosophy for Plato. But
since this is so, philosophy must speak to practical men, and
show them the true good, otherwise it would be no monument to such a man. For in Socrates there culminated the
ancient Greek conception of philosophy as a way of life, not
merely of thought in abstraction from life. It did not, however, take the form of a life apart from men, as in the
Pythagorean community (precursor in some respects of the
Christian Brotherhoods). The way of Socrates was that of
the greatest religious teachers moving amongst men of all
kinds and occupations, and endeavouring to arouse in them
the dormant thought of the meaning of their doings, a clearer
understanding of the purposes they professed. His method
was to convince them of ignorance, his faith that salvation
both of individual and of state could only come through a
knowledge that pierced the fog of self-conceit through which
life's possibilities were viewed by the majority. Thus virtue
would be knowledge, and here was the thought which Plato
laid hold of and which expanded in his hands, forced on by
its own power in the mind of the great Idealist, until the
knowledge which is virtue becomes knowledge of ultimate
good and truth, only completely attainable by the few. Here,
it appears (though there are distinguished scholars who
think otherwise), Plato left behind the actual Socrates, as he
lived and taught, always accessible to the wayfaring men,
and unwearied in zeal to show them a highway in which they
should not err. The meaning however of the Socratic dictum,
as applied in Xenophon's *Memorabilia*, is carried on into the
whole moral teaching of Plato. We do not drop the principle
that nothing but knowledge of our own limitations and our
own vocations, whether as shoemakers, sculptors, or statesmen, will enable us to do well and serve the community in
these capacities, though we have to recognise that, without

the authority of the wise who alone have the vision of the good, the plain man may err in his choice of task. And this is the assumption of Plato's most practical dialogues, notably the *Republic.*

In a general sense all the chief thinkers of Greece are at one on this question of the place of reason and knowledge in the good life. Because they defined the good as "the object of all men's striving"—indeed (as Aristotle especially conceives), the striving of the whole organic world—it must follow that all would take the course that led to it, if they could only know. The great and baffling problem was that humanity is endlessly inventive in the false goods it sets up. It ceaselessly pursues phantoms, and the good is hid from its eyes. Hence the problem of ethics, the cure of this soul-blindness, the destruction of illusions. And this can only be done by the instrument of knowledge. To the analysis and determination of this notion of knowledge for practical life, each of the three great thinkers contributed the interpretation belonging to his individual genius. The principle that self-knowledge is the beginning of all wisdom, is pre-eminently Socratic. It was vividly introduced as the precept of the Delphic Oracle, since the saying that Socrates was the wisest of men could only mean that he knew his own ignorance. His task in life henceforth was to win others over to this indispensable principle of moral education, so as to save them and their city from the calamities of ignorant leadership and ignorant labour. But that this principle is not discoverable by any merely logical or scientific demonstration is clearly shown as in a parable by the personal method of Socrates. He attracts by his sympathy with men, he arouses them by his spiritual power, to the consciousness that (as Callicles observes in Plato's *Gorgias*)—" If Socrates is right, the lives of most of us are upside down." Whether or not the allusions to the " divine sign " which warned

Socrates indicate a touch of the mystic in him, his influence must have proceeded from a spiritual force of personality.

In Plato the doctrine of virtue as knowledge has its finest expression in the place given to truth in his practical philosophy. Only in his latest work, the *Laws,* does he definitely treat truth as the fundamental virtue: " Truth is the beginning of every good thing." But the spirit of his whole philosophy is in these words. A tireless prophet of the reality of the ideal or the spiritual, and the shadowy existence of the things that are seen and perishable, he applies this thought with all its far-reaching significance and winged power to the problem of practical life. Truth in the soul is the one thing needful, the truth which purges the eye of the mind for the sight of the realities of life. Not the phantoms of ambition, pursuit of power, wealth, pleasure, can satisfy the universal hunger and thirst for the good. For the reality is the good as truth, beauty, harmony, and only the lie in the soul creates this delusion, that it will find its well-being in anything else. With this conviction of ideal reality, Plato combined a power, unrivalled in philosophy, of comprehending and describing realistically the forces that obscure the truth in the mind of the majority. In his dialogues the confusing and bewitching effects of the common passions, the impressionability to flattery and popular adulation to which the youth of gifted disposition is particularly prone, are laid bare by a master in the understanding of human nature. With a tragic irony he reveals the man most envied of his fellows for his power as tyrant to oppress and take from life all its sweets, as the most miserable of beings, and with poetic justice the just man persecuted and misunderstood to the end is seen to be in happier case. In Plato's judgment the monster evil, to the battle with which he devoted his unique powers of dialectic and moral indignation, was as it were expressed and personified in the Sophist and Sophistry.

Against this enemy, which he regarded as a deadly poison in the life of the people, he directed attacks hardly less scathing than the denunciations of the Pharisees by a greater teacher. The conflict is best understood as the eternal struggle between the single-minded and the double-minded vision and action in life. To the prophet of reality and soldier of truth it will always seem that the evil he combats has risen to a gigantic head in those who at the moment are leading the forces of compromise in whatever guise, and are demonstrating that there is a broad way and a wide gate for the pursuit of the prizes of the world, and no better prizes for the soul of man. The dark picture of the Sophists may have seemed to the genial men of the world as overdrawn as no doubt did the condemnation of the Pharisees to a similar class amongst the Jews. The Sophist is always with us; it is indeed, as Plato recognises, the voice of the world which is the greatest sophistry; but woe to those who speak in the voice of the world when they stand up as teachers and should be speaking the very truth. They are, in fact, to apply the doctrine of Plato's allegory of education, like men who come amongst prisoners in a dark cave as though to set them free, and, instead of striking off their fetters and enabling them to rise and turn to the light, insist that the chains are a help, enabling them to keep their poise in the life which is really theirs, whilst the daylight (should they seek it) would only dazzle and blind. For Plato the beginning and end of education is the turning of the soul to the light, first the lesser light which shows the laws which regulate life to be bound up with all that the young mind honours and holds dear, later the light which illuminates the soul, giving it sight for the source of all good.

The cultivation of the rational faculties is an essential part, then, of moral as of intellectual education : the two aspects cannot be severed. When Plato allows himself to mount to the very height of his idealism, he reveals the onward advance of the intellectual faculty, until it attains an insight into the principle of all good, and all reality. And this is indeed a spiritual vision, but only reached at the price of most of the ordinary joys of life. Youth passes away in the austere toil after knowledge, a knowledge unattainable unless the intellectual labour goes on side by side with a scorn of all other delights, a moral progress involving rejection of every ordinary pleasure. And if this ardent climb of mind and soul be at length crowned with the incomparable vision, and the desire to behold this perfection in quietude for the rest of life clutch the spirit of the philosopher, even this last infirmity must be overcome. He must return to the confusing unrest of existence with his weaker comrades in the cave, in service of the state. For his state has educated him for this and demands that the finest powers of thought shall be consecrated to the rude task of the political missionary up to the threshold of old age.

Plato's conception of the union of knowledge and virtue is, as earlier noticed, far from the original Socratic treatment of this relation, whilst Aristotle's doctrine of the practical reason or wisdom of life is again far from that of Plato. It has been seen that Aristotle's analysis of virtue, as consisting in a mean or moderate state, had to be completed by the reference to a standard, namely that of reason, or the wise man, one who has insight in the sphere of practice. This Aristotelian conception of the spirit of reason, as a guide in the complex situations of life which never exactly conform to the typical cases for the realisation of the several virtues, is one of the chief examples of his broad and human treatment of ethics. We are introduced to the man of practical insight or perhaps " Wisdom of Life " as the finest product of the moral system. The nature endowed with virtuous capacities, well-disciplined in the habit of right action before

the age of developed reason, enlightened by training in regard
to the main forms of practical experience, and the kinds of
difficulties most frequently presented by life, accustomed to
look for principles and aim at the highest end, finally possesses its principle in itself. This we may infer from what
precedes the account of that one among the intellectual
virtues which is essentially practical, that quality which
enables a man " to deliberate well concerning what is good
and seemly for himself in regard to the whole of a good
life." It is closely connected with self-control, for it is this
and no mere mental acuteness which sustains the true view
of life. It is a power to recognise principles, but is especially
shown in the moral understanding of particular cases, for
here it is " the eye of the soul," only developed by experience
in moral virtue. The exact nature of moral intuition has
never been more acutely analysed, and in his account of this
faculty Aristotle seems to supply something absent from
Plato's system whilst still faithful to the conception that
virtue depends on a kind of knowledge. It is a contribution
which fits in with his special attitude to practice. More
tolerant than Plato to the ordinary interests of those who
would always get the best out of life, though a highly conceived best, Aristotle was concerned to show how every
possible situation may be well met. Similarly in his *Politics*
he gives counsel to the statesman in all types of states, however
far from the ideal, how to preserve them from disruption.
Plato, on the other hand, held that there were situations
from which the good man can only draw aside, states in which
there is no service he can do but to wait until the storm is past.

However far Greek philosophy of life may seem to have
travelled in passing from Plato's conception of the life directed
by the vision of eternity, to Aristotle's teaching of the insight into the little daily details which enables the truly
practical man to win perfection, there is in both the thought

in which the greatest result of Greek ethics is given. Man's reason if rightly used is fitted to know the good, the truth of the universe. It is the sufficient guide of life. Amazed and perplexed as they must be at the frequent failure of reason to rule, they do not doubt its authority and power, or that when men are faced with reality and able to see things as they are, they cannot fail. In the explanation of evil, then, they choose rather the paradox of unwilling blindness than the paradox of the rebel will.

The problem of the will is set by the Greeks in such a very different context from that in which it arises for modern ethics that it is often held that they did not face it. Their psychological analyses do not give the conative principle the place it has in modern psychology. The nearest approach to this in Plato is the active, the spirited element in the soul, which is analogous to the warrior class in the state. This he names by the word often used in Homer for the vital force which quits a man, or even an animal, at death. In Aristotle the will appears to consist in the combination of reason, and the emotional element, obedient to it in the rightly ordered disposition. The discussion in his *Ethics* of the nature of voluntary and involuntary action is taken up first and mainly from the standpoint of the judge in the law-court, of which the approval and disapproval of public opinion is a reflection or corroboration. If the judge must hold the accused responsible for his actions when acting in full consciousness of all the circumstances and without obvious compulsion, there need be no question of appeal to a tribunal which takes a deeper view of motive than the court of law, and sees " compulsion " exercised by some overwhelming emotion, or ignorance consisti :g in a pitiable dimness of moral vision. Ignorance of first principles is the most unforgivable sin. If a man is to be held responsible for virtuous actions, he must also be responsible for his wrong-doing. In this conclusion Aristotle might appear to pronounce in favour of free-will. But clearly his subtle mind is not envisaging the problem in its profounder aspects. The only hint he gives in this direction would suggest that he would here follow Plato. If, as he observes, it be objected that everything depends on a man's vision of the good, then he indeed is well-endowed who has this vision. In fact, freedom of the mind is all in all, and without it there is no possibility of the free elective will. The logical conclusion had already been drawn by Plato: " No one is voluntarily unjust," and the principle applied unflinchingly (in the *Laws*) to the theory of punishment as reformatory and not retributive. Was Plato then a rigid necessitarian? It may be said that, prior to the history of religious and post-Christian philosophical speculation on this subject, the question could not have had the meaning it has for us. It may also however be observed that Plato was aware that there remained a problem which he had not fully laid bare. This is indicated by his treatment of the subject of destiny in certain myths of the experiences of the soul in the world beyond. Here the soul is given an opportunity of choosing the conditions of her life in external circumstances in the next stage of existence, and the choice is free. The circumstances, however, will determine the character, and they who choose the tyrant's power cannot escape the tyrant's vices and misery. Thus does Plato, as is his wont, adopt the mythical device, possibly to hint at a truth which he cannot demonstrate but would incline to believe. " Something," as Aristotle puts it, " does rest with ourselves." And here, with that large wisdom which may lead to silence on the most bitterly insistent questions, the greatest minds of Greece leave the matter.

Of the difficulty of the just life, as we have noticed, Plato was more acutely conscious than Aristotle. Neither

has any doubt that it is essentially natural for man, the
fulfilment of his own function, the health of the soul, in
the Platonic phrase, the energy of his highest and truest
being, or the activity of reason according to Aristotle. But
that there is a dualism in human nature Plato also affirms
in some of his most lofty passages and solemn situations.
Never forgetful of the martyrdom of Socrates, possessed
of the thought of the world's ignorance of its greatest men,
and the things which belong to its peace, he adopts in
the *Phaedo* the tone of the Orphic ascetic and conceives the
life of the spirit as in sharpest opposition to life in the world.
What Plato has in mind, however, is always an intellectual
religious opposition to the sensuous experience, confusing
alike to the pursuit of truth, and the purity of the single-
minded life. The philosophic tragedy of Plato's youth
deepened in his many-sided genius the influence of that
phase of Greek ethical history which was expressed in the
greatest works of the drama. He knew that life means
sacrifice and suffering, and he conceived of the highest type
of humanity as a man either rejected by his fellows or, if
he could, almost against hope, create a state harmonious
with his purposes, sacrificing his own best life, more blest
than his people can know, to their service. To a world of
thought which seems here poles asunder from Plato's belongs
Aristotle's picture of the hero of practical life, fully endowed
with goods of the soul and body, and with fortune's favours.
The soul's good is indeed still the one thing needful, but it
requires for its perfection these attendant advantages. In
spite of Aristotle's large humanity, the great citizen of the
Ethics, the magnanimous or high-souled man fully conscious of his own worth, is not an altogether attractive figure.
But if we take him as a type in which the Greek ideal is
expressed from an inner-worldly point of view, the study is
most illuminating. The Socratic principle of self-knowledge

may seem somewhat degraded when presented as un-shakable conviction of merit, but Aristotle is perhaps only carrying the principle to its logical outcome in one direction, in the view intended. The great personality with great responsibilities must, if society is to get the most out of his presence, be aware of his powers to do greatly. Plato's Socrates probed more truly the weakness of ordinary human nature in applying the doctrine mainly to the consciousness of ignorance and limited capacity. Perhaps indeed he almost approached a deeper truth, the sense of human finitude, in relation to the infinite.

If the Greek ideal in its narrower or more provincial aspect has slight appeal for us, when personified in the man of lofty soul whose loftiness carries with it a genial contempt for those who lack his advantages, this narrower conception attains all the beauty and power possible to it in Aristotle's treatment of " friendship." It is in his study of this, the finest flower of the rational life in society, that all the strength of Aristotle's more limited view of the moral ideal is expressed. At the same time he comes nearest to Plato's teaching, that the highest fruits of personal culture are a debt to the state. Neither philosopher knew of " human brotherhood " or the " love of humanity." The greater spiritual crises of the world which produced in the Stoic the conviction of an equality more important than all the inequalities of mankind, and in the Christian a bond of union beside which all causes of division must vanish, were not for them. Their understanding of the power that increases a thousandfold with co-operation as the torch is passed in brightening glow from hand to hand led them all the more to a faith in friendship as the means of drawing the best fruits from human association. The Platonic dialogues reveal the method of " team work " in the sphere of thought, and the discovery of truth, but Plato also shows in the political sphere (especially in the *Laws*) his belief that the citizen's life will be at its best if enriched by the joys of friendship. It is Aristotle, however, with his keener interest in completeness of life for the individual, his perception that "it may not be the same thing to be a good man as to be a good citizen," in any and every state, who depicts the life of friendship with the more loving care, and comes nearer to the conception of what a modern thinker (Royce) has termed "the beloved community" as the ideal. Friendship Aristotle regards as the virtue most necessary of all for life. "For no one would choose to live without friendship though he had all other goods." And because it seems to hold cities together, legislators are more zealous for friendship than for justice. The aspect of friendship as unanimity or harmony is its value for the political society. A deep truth of social philosophy is thus expressed by Aristotle in the special form suggested by Greek experience. Justice, he doubtless knew, depends, even more than the easier virtue of benevolence, on imagination; and how, as we may suppose him to ask, is imagination to have power except when exercised upon the little circle of beings akin to ourselves in outlook and experience? But even here, as is more evident in the cold scientific analysis in his *Politics* of the forms of actual states, and the difficulty of preserving them from ceaseless strife and faction, he had little favourable experience to which to point. His knowledge, however, of human nature shows him one only way to a better state of things, namely the development of a desire for the common good amongst men who loved the community as consisting of friends. Further he could not go without the religion of love. And the limitations of his standpoint are the more evident when we remember that his best state is built upon the institution of slavery, though he will not justify this except on the assumption that some are "slaves by nature," in this standpoint rising above his age. But, as has been finely argued by T. H. Green, our debt to the Greek moralists lies in their profound analysis of the nature of good, or value, whilst modern progress has largely consisted in the extension of the area, or idea of the community of mankind, amongst whom the good is to be realised.

This estimate has few better illustrations than the treatment of the principle of justice by the philosophers. The consideration of this virtue by Aristotle may still serve as an excellent introduction to the subject. We see that it must present itself in the same main outlines, and containing the same inner sources of conflict, whenever men begin to exercise their reason upon the divergent and confused ideas of right and wrong which have evolved from the primitive law of vengeance and notion of desert. The voice of reason speaks when Aristotle declares that the just is the equal. He strives to reconcile this with the deep conviction expressed in the law of retaliation. Corrective justice will strive to restore equality where wrong has been done by compelling the offender to compensate. Above all Aristotle recognises that justice in the individual, ethical justice, is constituted by his intention. The involuntary action is neither just nor unjust. And in his exposition of the supreme spirit of justice in " Equity," he gives expression to an ideal of the righteous man which soars above the ordinary Greek view. He is the person who exceeds in virtue, going beyond the requirements of the law. He introduces the temper of pity and forgiveness.

But Aristotle, if we take his practical philosophy as a whole, in spite of the optimistic tone of the ethics, hardly seems to conceive the reign of justice as truly realisable amongst men. Plato had attacked the problem in a more revolutionary way. It is not only the possibility of remodelling existing forms of society and strengthening known bonds of human nature. It is human nature itself which must be changed by the one and all but infallible expedient of finding for the soul its own task, its special vocation, its true life. Plato's thought in defining justice as the doing by every individual of his own thing may seem unpractical when we survey history and experience. It may, on the other hand, appear most profoundly practical if we view it as the single change which his deep insight saw to be sufficient to create the harmonious state and ordered soul. As such it provides an unerring standard for the criticism of life and human institutions, and suggests the form in which Plato might have developed a philosophy of personality had he envisaged this problem in the modern way.

In the later phases of classic Greek thought we pass into what is almost a new world. Much that has been dwelt upon as most characteristic of the Greek genius has vanished. And yet these phases are essentially Greek, and necessary to complete the impression of the universality of the Greek spirit. It could not cease to be creative without bringing forth examples, or at least foreshadowings, of all the great types of interpretation of life possible to man. We feel this especially when we consider the place of Stoicism in the history of Greek thought. Stoicism in a broad sense may be termed an attitude to life which naturally arises in the tragic ages of history. By a tragic age is here intended an age pervaded by the dread lest the values hitherto achieved and realised by the human spirit may be lost. In face of such a fear a particular quality of strength and resolution is developed which drives men back upon themselves. They are constrained to seek in the mind of man that good which in happier epochs seems streaming in upon them from society and the world in an endless wealth of values. But such an extreme subjectivity can provide no resting-place. Ethics itself must wither if no source can be found for the moral

c

ideal which presents itself with such power to the individual consciousness. The Stoic then, failing to discern what he needs in any lesser whole, turns to the greatest he can conceive. It is the universe to which he belongs in which he must find that harmony with his noblest thoughts which he pursues in vain in the history and organisations of mankind. And it is from thence that all the best in himself must be derived. For there is no other source, and it is moreover inconceivable that the whole should have less perfection than the parts. Thus does a more individualistic standpoint develop together with a more universalistic. In spite of the universality of their genius, which gives their philosophy of life a truth for all types of human experience, the practical teaching of Plato and Aristotle had, as we have seen, a close relation to the particular social forms which Greek life had produced. Hence the revolt, or rather perhaps the indifference to their philosophy, shown by the schools which followed in a period when the value of those social forms had been exhausted. Nevertheless Stoicism, at least in its Greek origin, is truly Greek. We may be apt to think of it as a view of life which is hardly a genuine product of the Greek spiritual experience. For how in that case could it have furnished to many of the Romans in an age more conscious of the tragedy of civilisation, their best consolation and guide? If we examine, however, the leading ideas which were transplanted to the Latin world of thought and there applied with all the Roman determination to the problem of spiritual endurance in a civilisation already showing signs of decay, we still find in them, in their changed setting, the stamp of the Greek genius and the outcome of Greek thought, especially in their treatment by the greatest of the later Stoics.

The philosophy on which Marcus Aurelius and Epictetus base moral teachings and reflections which have been felt to be the closest approach in philosophy to the spirit of

Christian ethics is still the philosophy of the Stoa, from which they take four or five great principles as an unshakable rock on which to stand. The individual must think of his life as an infinitesimal member of a great and perfect whole whose perfection resides in the whole and not the parts. This whole is animated by universal mind or God, and the individual, however insignificant his individuality, has the sublime quality of sharing in this all-pervading mind. The kinship of all mankind, through this highest possible bond, the freedom of perfect submission to the rule of that reason which is also his own, whether illuminating his path as the extreme idealism of duty, or obscurely presented in the inexorable laws of nature, the consistency of the imperturbable mind in all things—from such principles the spiritual genius of a Marcus Aurelius could draw the loftiest ethic and consolation. The harsher implications of earlier Stoicism, the almost impassable gulf between the wise and the unwise, the tendency to " Apathy " in relation to the feelings which may be a danger to strength of mind, are seen not to be inseparable from it.

Still, Marcus Aurelius is hardly, perhaps, the typical Stoic, and if the passages selected from his *Reflections addressed to Himself* are compared with the fragments from the accounts of early Greek Stoics, we may receive the impression of a subtle change of feeling which almost passes at times into a change of thought. The spirit of Epictetus is nearer to that of the rugged utterances handed down to us by various commentators as representing the views of Zeno, Cleanthes, Chrysippus and their followers, but it must be borne in mind that their philosophy may not be fully presented in these fragments.

The Roman Stoics are heirs to the Greek spirit also in their practice of the view of philosophy as a " Way of Life." In one form this principle culminates in the Stoic Emperor, though if we compare his application of it with that of Socrates, we feel that whilst the Greek laboured to introduce philosophy as the supreme good into the life of his fellow-men, the Roman, in his more difficult battle with life, felt his own task impossible without philosophy. The other greatest Roman Stoic, Seneca, is not represented in this book on Greek Thought, as he is less Greek in his spirit and did not express himself in Greek—an important point, I think, for the spirit of his writings.

The Epicurean philosophy, not less than the Stoic, bears marks of its origin in an age of disenchantment. But whereas this disenchantment seems in its effect on the Stoic to involve a fresh appeal to the human spirit to put forth all its strength in the swim, as it were, against the tide, with the Epicurean it becomes a sedative leading to a less exalted conception of life and duty. Also, driven in upon himself, he does not find his consolation in the conviction that "having nothing" he has "all," since the mind when most deprived of external goods knows itself to be akin to the universal source of true good. But he discovers that all conceptions of good are illusory except the good of an untroubled soul in a healthy body. Such a creed nobly interpreted, as it is by its founder, Epicurus himself, may come very near to Stoicism in some of its moral applications. But the doctrine of good as pleasure alone, and the treatment of pleasure and the absence of pain as the all-sufficient criterion, justify the place given to Epicurus as founder of Hedonism in the modern sense. His insistence, indeed, on the pleasures of the mind as the true pleasures and on the necessity of virtue to the happy life may not be altogether consistent with this place, but it is an inconsistency analogous to that of John Stuart Mill's view of higher and lower pleasures. We have to remember that our sources for the philosophy of Epicurus are again somewhat scanty.

The moral conceptions of Stoicism and Epicureanism respectively in their most obvious aspect present sharply the opposition of theories of duty and pleasure. In this light the last contribution of the undiluted Greek spirit to the history of moral ideas is to bring out in clearest relief the conflict which underlies a great part of moral reflection in modern philosophy. But perhaps it is better to see in the Epicurean ideal of life as an untroubled serenity, and the Stoic principle of calm acquiescence in all which happens in the divinely ordered course of things, at their best twin aspects of the reflection of a great people in the last true period of its history, having experienced greatly, still capable of giving mankind thoughts of value in all situations, if with less genius than of old.

.   .   .   .   .   .

It will be evident from the choice of the passages that the purpose of this book has been interpreted as especially to present illustrations as adequate as possible of the greatest period of Greek philosophical Ethics, that is, the period of Plato and Aristotle. The aim, however, has of course also been to illustrate the development of Greek ethical reflection, including the pre-philosophic tendencies. The complaint of Theognis that the just man constantly meets with evil fortune and the assumption of Hesiod that the just will always prosper are equally met by the conviction of Marcus Aurelius that the only things that are really good are in our own power, and beyond fortune whether good or ill. It is, of course, also the answer of Plato and of all spiritual ethics.

Since Mr. Cornford's book on *Greek Religious Thought*, in the present series, includes many passages suitable also as ethical illustrations, it has seemed best—where the choice is so wide—to avoid duplication as far as possible. The most important passages omitted on this account are the speech of Aeschylus' *Prometheus* illustrating the Greek understanding of the idea of sacrifice and suffering for the good of humanity, certain passages from Plato's *Phaedo* and *Phaedrus,* and Herodotus' narration of Solon's description of a life of happiness. On the other hand, a few passages which seemed essential appear here as well as in *Greek Religious Thought.*

CONTENTS

xxxix

CONTENTS

GREEK ETHICAL THOUGHT

HOMER

The *Iliad* and the *Odyssey* are thought by modern scholars to
have been chosen out of a mass of other ancient epic material, as
the Homeric Poems, for recitation at the Panathenaea Festival,
from the time of its institution by Pisistratus [1] (about 560 B.C.).

In reading Homer we often feel that we are in a pre-moral world,
or a society, in which the moral consciousness as we know it is
undeveloped. Nevertheless the Homeric epic is full, not merely of
the joy of life, but of rejoicing in the real value of life, the ideal
aspect with which man as soon as he is truly man colours all the
main human experiences. Thus home life, family love, friendship,
shine in this radiant poetry, beside much that no poetry can deprive
of its barbaric character for us. And above all, the duty and privilege
of hospitality and consolation for the stranger and suppliant, dear
to God, are insisted upon and expressed with a tenderness, beauty
and pathos hardly excelled elsewhere. For the individual the conviction of unalterable and incalculable Fate stimulates and fires
the resolve to make as glorious as possible the life which is as
uncertain as the frailest thing on earth.

ILIAD

Greek Text: edition by Walter Leaf, Litt.D., second edition.
Translation by George Chapman (1559–1634).

Home Affection

Hector, Andromache and Astyanax, ILIAD vi. 394 (Greek text).

SHE at his sight made breathless haste to meet him; she
, whose grace
Brought him with all so great a dower; she that of all the
race
Of King Aetion only lived; Aetion whose house stood
Beneath the Mountain Placius, environed with the wood of
Theban Hypoplace, being court to the Cialian land.

[1] See *The Rise of the Greek Epic*, by Gilbert Murray.

I

She ran to Hector, and with her tender of heart and hand
Her son, borne in his nurse's arms, where like a heavenly sign
Compact of many golden stars the princely child did shine.
Hector, though grief bereft his speech, yet smil'd upon his joy.
Andromache cried out, clasped hands, and to the strength of
    Troy
Thus wept forth her affection: " O noblest in desire!
Thy mind, inflam'd with others' good, will set thyself on fire.
Nor pitiest thou thy son, nor wife, who must thy widow be
If now thou issue; all the field will only run on thee.
Better my shoulders underwent the earth, than thy decease,
For then would earth bear joys no more; then comes the
    black increase
Of grief."
    .   .   .   .   .   .

        To this great Hector said:
" Be well assured, wife, all these things in my kind cares are
    weighed.
But what a shame, and fear, it is to think how Troy would
    scorn
That I should cowardly fly. The spirit I first did breathe
Did never teach me that; much less, since the contempt of
    death
Was settled in me, and my mind knew what a worthy was,
Whose office is to lead in fight, and give no danger pass,
Without improvement. In this fire must Hector shine.
Here must his country, father, friends in him be made divine.
And such a stormy day shall come (in mind and soul I know)
When sacred Troy shall shed her towers, for tears of over-
    throw;
When Priam, all his birth and power, shall in those tears be
    drown'd.
But neither Troy's posterity so much my soul doth wound,
Priam, nor Hecuba herself nor all my brothers' woes

(Who though so many and so good must all be food for foes),
As thy sad state; when some rude Greek shall lead thee weep-
      ing hence,
These free days clouded, and a night of captive violence
Loading thy temples, out of which thine eyes must never see,
But spin the Greek wives webs of task, and their fetch-
      water be
To Argos, from Messeides, or clear Hyperia's spring;
Which howsoever thou abhor'st, Fate's such a shrewish thing
She will be mistress; whose curst hands, when they shall
      crush out cries
From thy oppressions (being beheld by other enemies),
Thus they will nourish thy extremes: ' This dame was
      Hector's wife,
A man that, at the wars of Troy, did breathe the worthiest
      life
Of all their army.' This again will rub thy fruitful wounds,
To miss the man that to thy bands could give such narrow
      bounds.
But that day shall not wound mine eyes; the solid heap of
      night
Shall interpose, and stop mine ears against thy plaints and
      plight!"
This said, he reached to take his son who, of his arms
      afraid,
And then the horse-hair plume, with which he was so
      overlaid,
Nodded so horribly, he cling'd back to his nurse and cried.
Laughter affected his great sire, who doft and laid aside
His fearful helm, that on the earth cast round about it light,
Then took and kissed his loving son, and (balancing his
      weight
In dancing him) these loving vows to living Jove he used
And all the other bench of Gods: " O you that have infused

Soul to this infant, now set down this blessing on his star;—
Let his renown be clear as mine; equal his strength in war;
And make his reign so strong in Troy, that years to come may
    yield
His deeds and his fame, when rich in spoils he leaves the
    conquered field
Sown with his slaughters: ' These high deeds exceed his
    Father's worth.'
And let this echoed praise supply the comforts to come forth,
Of his dear Mother with my life." This said, the heroic sire
Gave him his mother; whose fair eyes fresh streams of love's
    salt fire
Billowed on her soft cheeks, to hear the last of Hector's
    speech,
In which her vows comprised the sum of all he did beseech,
In her wished comfort. So she took into her loving breast
Her husband's gift, who mov'd to see her heart so much
    opprest.
He dried her tears, and thus desired: " Afflict me not, dear
    wife,
With these vain griefs. He doth not live that can disjoin my
    life,
And this firm bosom, but my fate; and fate whose wings can
    fly?
Noble, ignoble fate controls; Once born, the best must die."
                           GEORGE CHAPMAN.

Noblesse Oblige—Sarpedon and Glaucus

ILIAD xii. 302.

    "What's brave, what's noble, let's do it, and make death proud to
take us."—SHAKESPEARE.

As ye see a mountain lion fare
Long kept from prey, in forcing which his high mind makes
    him dare,

Assault upon the whole full fold, though guarded never so
With well-armed men, and eager dogs, away he will not go,
But venture on and either snatch a prey or be a prey;
So fared divine Sarpedon's mind, resolved to force his way
Through all the fore fights and the wall; yet since he did not
 see
Others as great as he in name, as great in mind as he,
He spake to Glaucus: " Glaucus say, why are we honoured
 more
Than other men of Lycia in place; with greater store
Of meats and cups, with goodlier roofs; delightsome
 gardens; walks,
More lands and better; so much wealth, that court and
 country talks
Of us and our possessions, and every way we go
Gaze on us as we were their Gods? This where we dwell
 is so;
The shores of Xanthus ring of this and shall we not exceed
As much in merit as in noise? Come, be we great in deed
As well as look; shine not in gold, but in the flames of fight,
That so our neat-arm'd Lycians may say: ' See these are
 right
Our kings, our rulers, these deserve to eat and drink the best;
These govern not ingloriously; these thus exceed the rest,
Do more than they command to do.' O friend, if keeping
 back
Would keep back age from us, and death, and that we might
 not wrack
In this life's human sea at all, but that deferring now,
We shunned death ever, nor would I half this vain valour
 show
Nor glorify a folly so, to wish thee to advance,
But since we must go, though not here, and that besides the
 chance,

Proposed now there are infinite fates of other sort in death
Which neither to be fled nor 'scaped a man must sink beneath,
Come try me if this sort be ours, and either render thus
Glory to others, or make them resign the like to us."

GEORGE CHAPMAN.

The Sacredness of the Suppliant

Achilles and Priam, ILIAD xxiv. 477. Priam, the aged king of
Troy, comes to Achilles, slayer of his heroic son Hector, to petition
for Hector's body for burial with honour in Troy.

A great time Achilles gazed upon
His wondered-at approach, the rest did nothing see
While close he came up, with his hands fast holding the
    bent knee
Of Hector's conqueror, and kissed that large manslaughtering
    hand
That much blood from his sons had drawn. And as in some
    strange land,
And great man's house, a man is driven (with that abhorr'd
    dismay
That follows wilful bloodshed still his fortune being to slay
One whose blood cries aloud for his) to plead protection,
In such a miserable plight as frights the lookers-on;
In such a stupefied estate Achilles sat to see
So unexpected, so in right, and so incredibly
Old Priam's entry. All his friends one or another stared
To see his strange looks, seeing no cause. Thus Priam then
    prepared
His son's redemption: "See in me, O God-like Thetis' son,
Thy aged Father; and perhaps even now being out-run
With some of my woes, neighbour foes (thou absent) taking
    time
To do him mischief; no man left to terrify the crime
Of his oppression; yet he hears thy graces still survive

And joys to hear it, hoping still to see thee safe arrive
From ruin'd Troy; but I, cursed man, of all my race shall live
To see none living. Fifty sons the deity did give
My hopes to live in; all alive when near our trembling shore
The Greek ships harbour'd, nineteen of those sons one
    woman bore.
Now Mars a number of their knees hath strengthless left;
    and he
That was, of all, my only joy, and Troy's sole guard, by thee,
Late fighting for his country, slain; whose tendered person
    now
I come to ransom. Infinite is that I offer you,
Myself conferring it, exposed alone to all your odds,
Only imploring right of arms. Achilles! Fear the Gods,
Pity an old man like thy sire; different in only this,
That I am wretcheder, and bear that weight of miseries
That never man did, my cursed lips enforced to kiss that hand
That slew my children." This moved tears; his father's name
    did stand,
Mentioned by Priam, in much help to his compassion,
And moved Aeacides so much, he could not look upon
The weeping father. With his hand he gently put away
His grave face. Calm remission now did mutually display
Her power in either's heaviness. Old Priam, to record
His son's death and his deathsman see, his tears and bosom
    poured
Before Achilles; at his feet he laid his reverend head.
Achilles' thoughts, now with his sire, now with his friend,
    were fed.
Betwixt both sorrow filled the tent. But now Aeacides
(Satiate at all parts with the ruth of their calamities)
Started, and up he raised the king. His milk-white head and
    beard
With pity he beheld, and said: " Poor man, thy mind is scared
D

With much affliction. How durst thy person thus alone
Venture on his sight, that hath slain so many a worthy son,
And so dear to thee? Thy old heart is made of iron. Sit,
And settle we our woes, though huge, for nothing profits it.
Cold mourning wastes but our lives' heats. The Gods have
 destinate
That wretched mortals must live sad; 'tis the immortal
 state
Of Deity that lives secure."

GEORGE CHAPMAN.

Destiny

ILIAD xix. 397. Achilles' horse Xanthus foretells his destined end.

The fight's seat last, Achilles took behind;
Who looked so arm'd as if the sun, there fallen from heaven,
 had shined,
And terribly thus charged his steeds: " Xanthus and Balius,
Seed of the Harpy, in the charge ye undertake of us,
Discharge it not as when Patroclus ye left dead in field,
But when with blood for this day's fast observed revenge
 shall yield
Our heart satiety, bring us off." Thus, since Achilles spake
As if his awed steeds understood, 'twas Juno's will to make
Vocal the palate of the one; who, shaking his fair head
(Which in his mane, let fall to earth, he almost buried),
Thus Xanthus spake: " Ablest Achilles, now, at least, our
 care
Shall bring thee off, but not far hence the fatal minutes are
Of thy grave ruin. Nor shall we be then to be reproved,
But mightiest Fate, and the great God. Nor was thy best
 beloved
Spoiled so of arms by our slow pace, or courage's empair;
The best of Gods, Latona's son, that wears the golden hair,

Gave him his death's wound; though the grace he gave to
    Hector's hand.
We, like the spirit of the west, that all spirits can command
For power of wing, could run him off; but thou thyself
    must go,
So fate ordains; God and a man must give thee overthrow."
This said, the Furies stopped his voice. Achilles, far in rage,
Thus answered him: " It fits not thee, thus proudly to presage
My overthrow. I know myself it is my fate to fall
Thus far from Phthia; yet that fate shall fail to vent her gall
Till mine vent thousands." These words us'd, he fell to
    horrid deeds,
Gave dreadful signal, and forthright made fly his one-hoofed
    steeds.

GEORGE CHAPMAN.

ODYSSEY

Welcome for the Stranger and Suppliant

Greek Text: edited by J. Van Leeuwen and M. B. Mendes Da Costa
(Greek and English Loeb's Classics). Translation by George Chapman.
Odysseus comes as suppliant to the palace of Alcinous, and kneels
before Queen Arete. After petitioning for aid on his homeward
journey, he goes to the hearth and sits in the ashes.
    An old hero, Echineus, speaks.

ODYSSEY vii. 159.

     " Alcinous! It shows not decently,
     Nor doth your honour what you see admit,
     That this your guest should thus abjectly sit,
     His chair the earth, the hearth his cushion,
     Ashes as if appos'd for food. A throne,
     Adorned with due rites, stands you more in hand
     To see his person placed in, and command
     That instantly your heralds fill in wine,
     That to the God that doth in lightnings shine

We may do sacrifice; for He is there,
Where these his reverend suppliants appear.
Let what you have within be brought abroad,
To sup the stranger. All these would have showed
This fit respect to him, but that they stay
For your precedence, that should grace the way."

Some God may come in the Likeness of a Beggar and Suppliant

ODYSSEY xvii. 481. Antinous, the most insolent of Penelope's
wooers, insults Odysseus, disguised as an aged beggar, and hurls
a stool at him. Even the shameless wooers are shocked at this
treatment of a stranger and suppliant.

This made the rest as highly hate his folly,
As he had violated something holy.
When one, even of the proudest, thus began:
" Thou dost not nobly, thus to play the man
On such an errant wretch. O ill disposed
Perhaps some sacred Godhead goes enclosed
Even in his abject outside; for the Gods
Have often visited these rich abodes
Like such poor stranger pilgrims since their powers
(Being always shapeful) glide through towns and towers,
Observing, as they pass still, who they be
That piety love, and who impiety."

Father and Son

ODYSSEY xxiv. 231. Odysseus, after twenty years' absence, finds
his old father, Laertes, in solitude, unkempt, and working in a field.

Him when Ulysses saw consumed with age,
And all the ensigns on him that the rage
Of grief presented, he brake out in tears;
And, taking stand then where a tree of pears
Shot high his forehead over him, his mind
Had much contention, if to yield to kind,

Make straightway to his father, kiss, embrace,
Tell his return, and put on all the face
And fashion of his instant-told return;
Or stay the impulsion, and the long day burn
Of his quite loss given in his father's fear
A little longer, trying first his cheer
With some free dalliance, the earnest being so near.
    This course his choice preferr'd, and forth he went.

(They enter into conversation, and what Odysseus relates leads
Laertes to think he will never see his son again.)

314.
             This a cloud of grief
Cast over all the forces of his life.
With both his hands the burning dust he swept
Up from the earth, which on his head he heaped,
And fetched a sigh, as in it life were broke.
Which grieved his son, and gave so smart a stroke
Upon his nostrils with the inward stripe,
That up the vein rose there; and weeping-ripe
He was to see his sire feel such woe
For his dissembled joy; which now let go,
He sprung from earth, embraced and kissed his sire,
And said: " O father! He of whom ye enquire
Am I myself, that, from you twenty years,
Is now returned."

                    GEORGE CHAPMAN.

HESIOD

About the eighth century B.C., born at Ascra in Boeotia. His poems are the *Works and Days* and *Theogony*.
Greek Text: *Epics of Hesiod*, with an English Commentary by F. A. Paley, M.A. Translation by George Chapman.

The Praise of the Mean Life

WORKS AND DAYS 40.

O Fools that all things unto Judgment call
Yet know not how much half is more than all,
Nor how the mean life is the firmest still,
Nor of the mallow and the daffodil,
How great a good the little meals contain,
But God hath hid from men the healthful mean.
For otherwise a man might heap and play
Enough to serve the whole year in a day;
Nor move his labouring mules nor oxen yoke.

Justice brings Prosperity

WORKS AND DAYS 220.

But crooked justice jointly brings with it
Injurious perjury, and that unfit
Outrage bribed judges use, that makes them draw
The way their gifts go, ever cuts out law
By crooked measures. Equal justice then
All clad in air th' ill minds of bribed men
Comes after, mourning, mourns the city's ill.
But those that with impartial dooms extend
As well to strangers as their household friend
The law's pure truth, and will in no point stray
From forth the strait track of the equal way.

With such the cities all things noble nourish,
With such the people in their profits flourish,
Sweet peace along the land goes. Nor to them
All-seeing Jove will e'er allot th' extreme
Of baneful war. No hunger ever comes,
No ills, where judges use impartial dooms.
But goods well got maintain still neighbour feasts,
The fields flow there with lawful interest.
On hills the high oak acorns bears. In dales
Th' industrious bee her honey-sweet exhales:
And fleecy sheep are shorn with festival.

     .   .   .   .   .

238.

But whom rude injury delights and acts
That misery and tyranny contracts,
Far-seeing Jove for such predestines pain.
And oftentimes the whole land doth sustain
For one man's wickedness, that thriving in
Unequal dooms, gives judgment for his gain.
For where such men bear privileged office still,
There Jove pours down whole deluges of ill.
Famine and pestilence together go,
The people perish, women barren grow,
Whole houses vanish there, sometimes in peace
And sometimes armies raised to shield th' increase
The Gods late gave them, even those Gods destroy,
Their ramparts ruin, and let rapine joy
The goods injustice gathered, or elsewhere
Jove sinks their ships, and leaves their ventures there.

     .   .   .   .   .

263.

Observing this, ye gift-devouring Kings,
Correct your sentences, and to their springs
Remember ever to reduce those streams

Whose crooked courses every man condemns,
Whoever forgeth for another ill,
With it himself is overtaken still,
For ill, men run on that they most abhor.
Ill counsel worst is to the counsellor.
For Jove's eye all things seeing, and knowing all,
Even these things if he will of force must fall,
Within his sight and knowledge. Nor to him
Can these bribed Dooms in cities shine so dim,
But he discerns them and will repay them pain;
Else would not I live justly amongst men,
Nor to my justice frame my children,
If to be just is ever to be ill,
And that the unjust finds most justice still,
And Jove gave each man in the end his will.
But he that wields the lightning, I conceive
To these things thus, will no conclusion give.

285.

    ·   ·   ·   ·   ·

The just man's state shall in his seed exceed,
And after him breed honours as they breed.
But why men's ills prevail so much with them
I that the good know will the cause unfold,
O foolish Perses, wherefore with much ease
To vice and her love men may make access.
Such crowds in rout herd to her, and her court
So passing near lies, their way sweet and short.
But before virtue do the Gods rain sweat,
Through which with toil and weary-dragging feet
You must wade to her; her path long and steep,
And at your entry 'tis so sharp and deep;
But scaling once her height the joy is more
Than all the pain she put you to before.

GEORGE CHAPMAN.

EARLY LYRIC POETS

THEOGNIS

565–490 B.C.

Theognis, a poet of stormy times and many reverses of fortune, does not write in a very lofty strain. He was much preoccupied by the prosperity of the unjust and misfortunes of the just. In the following lines he maintains that the evil deed brings retribution, though it may be on the descendants of the wrongdoer, not himself.

Elegies of Theognis, Revised Text by T. Hudson-Williams, M.A., 1910. *Cf.* also *Poetae Minores Graeci*, ed. T. Gaisford, Vol. i. ΘΕΟΓΝΙΔΟΣ ΓΝΩΜΑΙ.

Evil brings Retribution

197–208.

Wealth which is the gift of heaven, justly acquired by man, and with pure hands, ever abides. But if wrongly and unduly with thoughts greedy of gain a man procure it or grasp by a false oath, for the moment indeed he seems to carry off some gain, but in the end evil is engendered. The mind of the Gods prevails. But the thoughts of men are deceived. For not on the offence itself falls the punishment of heaven though the doer himself atones for the evil, since a black fate he has forthwith hung over his dear children. The retribution did not overtake the other (*i.e.* the doer), for there came relentless death, holding the doom before his eyes.

(Elsewhere Theognis protests against the law (conceived to prevail) that the innocent should suffer for the sins of their ancestors.)

729–750.

Would, Father Zeus, that it were pleasing to the gods, and acceptable in their sight, that the insolence of the wicked should be noted and that he who recklessly works evil deeds

15

nor reverences the gods in aught, himself should thereafter atone for his wrong, neither the sins of the father hereafter bring woe upon the children. But that the children of an unjust father who purpose and do righteously, dreading thy wrath, O Son of Kronos, and from the first delight in righteous dealings with their fellow-citizens, should not pay for the transgression of their fathers—that this should be the will of the blessed Gods!

But as it is, he who does the deed escapes, and another bears the burden of ill.

And this, O King of the Immortals, how is it just— that the man who is far from unjust acts, neither holding to any trespass nor sinful oath, but lives uprightly, should not meet with justice?

Who among mortals, beholding these things, would there- after stand in dread of the Immortals, and what spirit will be his when the man who is unjust and wicked, fearing the wrath neither of man nor of gods, vaunts himself adorned with opulence, while the righteous are afflicted with distress and suffer in poverty?

Nature and Nurture

429.

To rear a child is an easier matter than to instil a noble disposition. For no one has yet devised the means to make the senseless sound in mind and the bad man good. If indeed God had given this power to the Asclepiads, to heal wickedness, and the perverse hearts of men, great the wages, large the reward they would have earned. But if the thought of the heart could be created and set in a man, never would a bad man have been born of a good father, but he would be obedient to the words of sober teaching. Through instruction, never wilt thou make the evil good.

SIMONIDES

556–467 B.C.

The spirit of Simonides' poetry is thought to be noblest in Greek lyric poetry.
From the Greek of Professor Mackail's *Select Epigrams from the Greek Anthology.*

Epitaphs

The Athenian Dead at Plataea

If to die nobly is the greatest part of virtue, on us of all men Fortune has bestowed this lot. For on our swift way to cast about Greece the raiment of freedom we lie, possessed of an undecaying glory.

The Lacedaemonian Dead at Plataea

These men when they had cast undying fame
On their loved land, themselves then wrapped around
Dark clouds of death. Yet dead they are not found
To die, for virtue from above in praise
Uplifts beyond the House of Death, their name.

The Spartans who fell at Thermopylae

These tidings, stranger, to the Spartans bear,
That here we lie at rest, and this the cause,
Obedience to their laws.

BACCHYLIDES

PROBABLY 507–428 B.C.

The *Odes* of Bacchylides, celebrating victories in the Great Athletic Contests of Greece, are characterised by the moral reflections he introduces from time to time.

The Glory of Virtue

ODES OF VICTORY i. 48–74. From Jebb's Edition of the *Poems and Fragments of Bacchylides*, Greek and English.

The best glory is that of Virtue, so deem I now and ever: wealth may dwell with men of little worth, and will exalt the spirit; but he who is bountiful to the gods can cheer his heart with a loftier hope. If a mortal is blessed with health, and can live on his own substance, he vies with the most fortunate. Joy attends on every state of life, if only disease and helpless poverty be not there. The rich man yearns for great things as the poorer for less; mortals find no sweetness in opulence, but are ever pursuing visions that flee before them. He whose mind is blown about by ambitions light as air, wins honour only for his lifetime. The task of virtue is toilsome; but when it has been duly wrought to the end, it leaves the enviable meed of bright renown, outlasting death.

Many Paths to Renown

ODES OF VICTORY iii. 35–52.

Men seek various paths which they shall tread to the winning of bright renown. And countless are the kinds of human knowledge. A man is rich in golden hope because he has wisdom, or has been honoured with the gifts of the

Graces, or has skill in some manner of soothsaying. Another aims his wily shaft at wealth, while some there be who take delight in the works of husbandry, and in herds of oxen. The future brings forth issues which cannot be judged beforehand, so as to tell how Fortune will incline the scale. The noblest lot for a man is that his own worth should make him widely admired among his fellows. I know also the mighty power of riches, which can clothe even the useless man with merit.

But wherefore have I turned my strain so far out of its due course?

R. C. JEBB.

AESCHYLUS

525–456 B.C.

As Mr. R. C. Trevelyan says in the Introduction to his translation of the *Oresteia,* "The fragments of Aeschylus' predecessors are too scanty to give us any idea of what he may have owed to them. But it seems probable that drama, as one of the supreme forms of art, was the creation of his own unique personal genius."

The Trilogy of Aeschylus known as the *Oresteia* may be interpreted in its moral meaning as a single drama of the development of the conception of justice from the primitive law of vengeance, evil for evil, continuing from generation to generation, towards a more liberal and humane principle. In the *Agamemnon* the older law prevails. In the *Choephori* the moral consciousness of the race, growing beyond the ancient law, carries out its behests, with suffering and remorse. In the *Eumenides,* the old and new conceptions are brought into direct conflict, and the ancient spirit represented by the avenging furies (Erinyes) gives way, passing into a milder and higher form as beneficent justice (the Eumenides). As elsewhere in Aeschylus, the value of suffering in bringing insight is emphasised.

Text: *Poetae Scenici Graeci ex Recognitione,* Guil. Dindorfii. Translation by Mr. R. C. Trevelyan.

Truth comes by Suffering

AGAMEMNON 176.

> Zeus, who into wisdom's way
> Guideth mortals, 'stablishing
> This decree: " By suffering Truth."
> Woes' aching memories before the mind
> Ooze in sleep drop by drop:
> So to men wisdom comes, without their will.

.   .   .   .   .

AGAMEMNON 250.

> As even-scaled Justice wills
> Those who suffer, learn the Truth. The future,
> Though ere it come, men may know it—let it be;
> 'Twere but to weep, ere 'tis need.

20

*Unrighteousness punished. Excess of Prosperity
dangerous*

AGAMEMNON 463.

Late or soon
Will the dark Erinyes doom
The man who thrives unrighteously
To waste and dwindle luckless down
Until his light be quenched: and once
Lost in the darkness, who shall help him?
In excess of glory is peril:
For on mortals overweening
Are the bolts of Zeus sped.

Only the Just blest

AGAMEMNON 751.

A proverb old framed by ancient wisdom saith
That a man's fortune once 'tis grown to highest pitch of
greatness,
Engendering, dies not childless ever;
For from the womb of prosperous hours
Unappeasable sorrow issueth.
But with such doctrine I hold not.
'Tis the deed of sin begetteth
In its own likeness a sequent
Generation of disaster.
None save the house of the just
Is ever blest in its children.

.   .   .   .   .   .

But Justice shines even beneath lowly roofs smoke-begrimed,
Honouring the righteous man;
And gold-bespangled palaces, where the hands are foul,
With averted eyes
Abandoning, she seeks fellowship with Innocence,

Flattering not the might of wealth,
False coin, stamped with men's praise,
All to an end she guideth.

Measure in Prosperity safest

AGAMEMNON 1001.

Verily Health grown over-great may not abide
Within narrow bounds. But a thin wall stays
Its neighbour Disease from encroaching.
So may the ship of a man's
Prosperous fate unawares
Strike on a reed of unseen disaster,
Yet if timely caution fling
Overboard excess of wealth
Jettisoned from Measure's sling,
Then the house with baleful store
Overladen shall not sink,
Foundering like a ship in storm.

Fate

AGAMEMNON 1299.

Kassandra. There is no escape, friends, none, when time
    is full—
Chorus Leader. Yes, but time's last hour still is found the best.
Kassandra. The day is come, little were gained by flight.

Retribution for the Individual

AGAMEMNON 1562.

Chorus. The spoiler is spoiled, the slayer pays reprisal.
    While on his throne Zeus abides, abides the truth:
    " Who doth the deed suffereth," so the law stands.

The Avenging Spirit may pause

AGAMEMNON 1654.

Klytemnestra.   Let us do no further ill,
Miseries are here to reap in plenty, a pitiable crop.
Harm enough is done already, let no blood by us be spilt.
Now 'tis time that thou and these should seek their
    dwellings each,
Ere some rash deed bring repentance—since we have
    come to such a pass.
Then if haply these afflictions prove enough, there let
    us stop,
Sorely smitten thus already by the heavy wheel of fate.
                              R. C. TREVELYAN.

Justice to render Evil for Evil

CHOEPHORI 307.

Chorus. O powerful Fates, let Zeus now send
Prosperous fortune
Unto us, whom righteousness aideth.
" Enmity of tongue for enmity of tongue
Be paid in requital," cries Justice aloud,
Exacting the debt that is owed her.
" Murderous blow for murderous blow
Let him take for his payment." " To the deed its reward."
So speaks immemorial wisdom.

Retribution a Moral Law to which the Gods must bow

CHOEPHORI 956.

Chorus. Even as Loxias without guile proclaimed
Out of the cavern vast of his Parnassian shrine,
So on the sin and the guile,
    E

That long here have reigned, Justice hath brought revenge.
A strict fate forbids divine power itself
To serve evil ends.
Revere then the law by which Heaven is bound.

R. C. TREVELYAN.

The Spirit of Justice rising above Vengeance

In the *Eumenides* the avenging Furies or Erinyes, who represent
the primitive conception of Justice as Vengeance, are persuaded
by Athena to become the equitable or beneficent divinities (Eumenides) and take up their abode at Athens, helping the prosperity
and peace of the city in this new character.

EUMENIDES 976.

Chorus. Let not fierce Faction's moan
Hungering after evil deeds
In this city e'er be heard.
Nor may the dust that has drunk the red blood of the
townsmen
In wrath grow vengeful,
Lusting for fresh bloodshed,
Payment for citizens slain.
Rather in loving kindness
May they rejoice one another,
And with one soul let them hate.
In such wise many human ills are cured.
Athena. Hear with what wise speech into the pathway of
blessings they enter.
Stern and terrible though they appear,
Great gain shall they bring you, people of Athens ;
If you repay them for kindness with kindness
And reverent worship, this shall your fame be,
To guide both your land
And city in the straight path of justice.

Man's Pitiful Estate

AGAMEMNON 1327.

Kassandra. Alas for man's estate! His happiness
Shows like a sketch a shadow: but his misery—
'Tis a picture by a wet sponge dashed clean out.
And this is the more pitiable by far.

CHOEPHORI 1017.

Chorus. No mortal man may pass his life
Without scathe, if he pay not in sorrow
Alas!
Woe must be, to-day or hereafter.

R. C. TREVELYAN.

SOPHOCLES

495–406 B.C.

The most ideal of Greek tragic poets. An Athenian, he was one of the generals in the Samian campaign, 440–439.

Vision comes through Suffering

OEDIPUS COLONEUS 73. Edition of R. C. Jebb, Greek and English. The blind and stricken Oedipus, led to Athens in his wanderings, guided by his daughter Antigone, knows that he will die there, and the city which is to receive him kindly will be blest on his account.

Stranger. And what help can be from one who sees not ?
Oedipus. In all that I speak there shall be sight.

Those who shelter the Stranger in Distress have the Fear of God

OEDIPUS COLONEUS 253–4.

Oedipus. What good comes then of repute or fair fame, if it ends in idle breath; seeing that Athens, as men say, has the perfect fear of Heaven, and the power, above all cities, to shelter the vexed stranger, and the power above all to succour him?

The Offering of the Pure Spirit acceptable

OEDIPUS COLONEUS 498–9.

Oedipus. For I think that one soul suffices to pay this debt for ten thousand if it come with good will to the shrine.

Succour to the Stranger

OEDIPUS COLONEUS 565–8.

Theseus. Never then would I turn aside from a stranger such as thou art now, or refuse to aid in his deliverance; for well I know that I am a man, and that in the morrow my portion is no greater than thine.

26

All Things are confounded by Time

OEDIPUS COLONEUS 607–15.

Oedipus. Kind son of Aegeus, to the gods alone comes never old age or death, but all else is confounded by all-mastering time. Earth's strength decays, and the strength of the body; faith dies, distrust is born; and the same spirit is never steadfast among friends, or betwixt city and city; for be it soon, or be it late, men find sweet turn to bitter, and then once more to love.

Pessimism

OEDIPUS COLONEUS 1225–38.

Chorus. Not to be born is past all prizing best; but when a man hath seen the light, this is next best by far, that with all speed he should go thither, whence he hath come.

For when he hath seen youth go by, with its light follies, what troublous affliction is strange to his lot, what suffering is not therein? Envy, factions, strife, battles and slaughters; and last of all, age claims him for her own,— age, dispraised, infirm, unsociable, unfriended, with whom all woe of woes abides.

R. C. JEBB

The Divine Law higher than the Law of the State

ANTIGONE. Edition, Greek and English, R. C. Jebb. Antigone refuses to obey the edict of King Creon (which ranks as a law of the state) forbidding anyone to render funeral rites to her dead brother Polyneices, killed in warfare against Thebes. She declares that in performing these rites she is obeying a higher law than that of the state, the divine law which has no human origin. There is no conflict of obligations for her, no hesitation, but the moral problem of apparently conflicting duties would be deeply felt by the Greeks who first saw Sophocles' play, and for whom the law of the state represented an obligation with sacred associations. This conflict is most vividly presented in Antigone's words at the beginning of the play:

"I shall rest 'sinless in my crime'" (JEBB).

446.

Creon. Now tell me thou—not in many words but briefly
—knewest thou that an edict had forbidden this?

Antigone. I knew it: could I help it? It was public.

Creon. And thou didst indeed dare to transgress that law?

Antigone. Yes; for it was not Zeus that had published me
that edict; not such are the laws set among men by the
Justice who dwells with the gods below; nor deemed I
that thy decrees were of such force that a mortal could
override the unwritten and unfailing statutes of heaven.
For their life is not of to-day or yesterday, but from all
time, and no man knows when they were first put forth.

R. C. JEBB.

Submission

AJAX. From the Greek, *Poetae Scenici Graeci ex Recognitione,*
Guil. Dindorfii. The impression of this passage (one of those which
disprove the view that the Greeks could not feel as profoundly as
the moderns the reverberation of their emotions in nature) is not
lessened by our knowledge that the teaching is not really accepted
by the insane speaker himself.

669.

Ajax. The most awful and the mightiest things submit.
Storms with their weight of wintry snow yield to fruitful
summer. The wheel of never-ending night gives way to
the white steeds of day kindling the light. The blast of
terrible winds ceasing, suffers the groaning sea to rest.
Even all-powerful sleep loosens the fetters it has bound, nor
holds fast for ever those it has in its clutch. How then
should we who know discern not the measured way?

EURIPIDES

480–406 B.C.

Born at Salamis, said to have written about ninety plays, of which nineteen survive. "Even if faulty in various ways, at any rate clearly the most tragic of the poets" (ARISTOTLE).

Greek Text: *Poetae Scenici Graeci*, Guil. Dindorfii. Translation: Professor Gilbert Murray.

Friendship

IPHIGENIA IN TAURIS 597.

Iphigenia offers Orestes (whom she does not yet know to be her brother) his life if he will bear a message for her to Argos. Pylades must remain as the sacrifice required by Artemis of all strangers who land on the island.

Orestes. Strange woman, as thou biddest let it be,
Save one thing. 'Twere for me a heavy weight
Should this man die. 'Tis I and mine own fate
That steers our goings. He but sails with me
Because I suffer much. It must not be
That by his ruin I should 'scape mine own,
And win thy grace withal. 'Tis simply done.
Give him the tablet. He with faithful will
Shall all thy hest in Argolis fulfil,
And I . . . who cares may kill me. Vile is he
Who leaves a friend in peril and goes free
Himself. And as it chances, this is one
Right dear to me; his life is as my own.

(Pylades appears to accept this in silence. Later, when Iphigenia has left them)—

674.

Pylades. I cannot live for shame if thou art dead.
I sailed together with thee; let us die
Together. What a coward slave were I,
Creeping through Argos and from glen to glen
Of wind-torn Phocian hills! And most of men—

29

For most are bad—will whisper how one day
I left my friend to die and made my way
Home. They will say I watched the sinking breath
Of thy great house and plotted for thy death
To wed thy sister, climb into thy throne . . .
I dread, I loathe it.—Nay, all ways but one
Are shut. My last breath shall go forth with thine,
Thy bloody sword, thy gulf of fire be mine
Also. I love thee and I dread men's scorn.
687.

Orestes. Peace from such thoughts! My burden can be borne;
But where one pain sufficeth, double pain
I will not bear. Nay, all that scorn and stain
That fright thee, on mine own head worse would be
If I brought death on him who toiled for me.

Love of Home

Iphigenia in Tauris 1094.
Chorus of captive Greek women.

Sister, I too beside the sea complain,
    A bird that hath no wing,
Oh for a kind Greek market-place again,
For Artemis that healeth woman's pain;
    Here I stand hungering,
Give me the little hill above the sea,
The palm of Delos fringed delicately, .
The young sweet laurel and the olive-tree
    Grey leaved and glimmering;
O Isle of Leto, isle of pain and love;
The Orbed water and the spell thereof;
Where still the Swan, minstrel of things to be,
    Doth serve the Muse and sing!

.   .   .   .   .   .

1137.

Ah me,
To rise upon wings and hold
Straight on up the steeps of gold
Where the joyous Sun in fire doth run
Till the wings should faint and fold
O'er the house that was mine of old:

Or watch where the glade below
With a marriage dance doth glow,
And a child will glide from her mother's side
Out, out where the dancers flow:
As I did long ago.

Oh, battles of gold and rare
Raiment and starrèd hair
And bright veils crossed amid tresses tossed
In a dusk of dancing air!
O Youth and the days that were!

GILBERT MURRAY.

Purity of Heart

HIPPOLYTUS 317.

Phaedra. My hand is clean; but is my heart, O God?

426-7.

Phaedra. 'Tis written, one way is there, one to win
This life's race, could man keep it from his birth
A true clean spirit.

The Sins of the Fathers

HIPPOLYTUS 1378.

O strange false curse! Was there some blood-stained head,
Some father of my line unpunishèd,
Whose guilt lived in his kin,

And passed, and slept, till after this long day
It lights—Oh why on me? me far away
      And innocent of sin?

Destiny

1435.

Artemis. And thou, Hippolytus, shrink not from the king,
   Thy father. Thou wast born to bear this thing.

GILBERT MURRAY.

Truth found among the Simple and hidden from the Wise

BACCHAE 425.

   Love thou the Day and the Night,
   Be glad of the Dark and the Light,
   And avert thine eyes from the lore of the wise.
   The simple nameless herd of Humanity
   Hath deeds and faith that are truth enough for me!

Wisdom

BACCHAE 877.

Chorus. What else is wisdom? What of man's endeavour
   Or God's high grace so lovely and so great?
   To stand from fear set free, to breathe and wait,
   To hold a hand uplifted over Hate
   And shall not Loveliness be loved for ever?

   O strength of God, slow art thou and still,
   Yet failest never!
   On them that worship the Ruthless Will,
   On them that dream doth His judgment wait,
   Dreams of the proud man making great
         And greater ever
   Things which are not of God.

GILBERT MURRAY.

ANAXIMANDER OF MILETUS

Said to have been born 610, and to have written his book about 546 B.C. The second Milesian Philosopher. He was a very bold and daring thinker, but although a moral element may be traced in the spirit of all the early Greek speculation, his philosophy is really concerned with the Nature of Things. The following fragment illustrates the notion of the limits which all things in nature, as in human existence, must observe, an idea pervading Greek thought.

The text from which the translation of this fragment and all those of Heraclitus, Philolaus and Democritus is made is that given in Diels' *Fragmente der Vor-Sokratiker*, and the reference to his numbering.

DIELS 9.

That from which all things derive their origin is also that to which they return, as their destruction, according to destiny. For they render justice and retribution to each other for their injustice, in conformity with the order of time.

Simplicius, from THEOPHRASTUS.

HERACLITUS OF EPHESUS

Said to have "flourished" 504–501 B.C. Wrote in an obscure style, and was named "the dark." His sayings have a prophetic ring, and seem to contain germs of much of later thought. Those which have been selected illustrate especially the ideas of the common Word or Reason, and of harmony through discord.

DIELS 2.

(92.) Therefore ought we to follow wisdom, that is the common. For wisdom is the common. But though the Word is common, the multitude live as if they had an insight of their own.

33

8.

(46.) The striving of opposites is beneficial and out of differences arises loveliest harmony, and all things come to be through strife

32.

(65.) That which is alone wisdom is one. It wishes and does not wish to be called by the name of God.

45.

(71.) The limits of soul thou would'st not find though thou should'st traverse every path; so deep a ground has it.

51.

(45.) They do not understand how though at discord with itself it (the One) accords with itself; harmony from contrary striving, as of the bow and the lyre.

53.

(44.) War is father of all things and king of all, and some he makes gods, and others men, and some he has made slaves and others free.

54.

(47.) Hidden harmony is better than harmony revealed.

60.

(69.) The way up and down is one and the same.

62.

(67.) Immortals mortals, mortals immortals, living each other's death, and dying each other's life.

67.

(36.) God is day and night, winter and summer, war and peace, plenty and hunger. But He changes Himself as the fire when it is mingled with smoke and has the name of each at pleasure.

102.

(61.) To God all things are beautiful and good and just. But men hold some things unjust, others just.

110.

(104.) Though the desires of all men were all fulfilled, it would not be better for them.

112.

(107.) Thought is the greatest excellence, and it is wisdom to speak truth and to do in accordance with nature.

PHILOLAUS

FIFTH CENTURY B.C.

A contemporary of Socrates, and one of the leading Pythagoreans. Their view of the soul is expressed in Plato's *Phaedo*.

The Soul

DIELS 14.

The ancient teachers of divine law and seers also bear witness that the soul has been yoked with the body as a punishment, and is buried in this as a tomb.

DEMOCRITUS OF ABDERA

Probably born about 460 B.C., said to have lived to a great age. Democritus, after Leucippus founded the Atomist philosophy, appears to have developed also ethical views, in which Epicurus followed him as well as in his materialistic system.

DIELS 3.

(163.) He who wishes to have a contented mind must not engage in many occupations, neither private nor public, nor in what he undertakes strive beyond his powers and nature; but he should be so watchful over himself that even when good fortune visits him and appears to raise him to the skies he does not regard it, and does not grasp what is beyond his power. For a moderate filling up (of the cup) is safer than an overflow.

4.

(34.) Democritus in his work on the end said that it was contentment which he called a stable state. And he often said that pleasure and pain is the criterion (of what is beneficial and not beneficial).

Sayings of Democritus

DIELS 40.

(15.) Neither physical strength nor money gives happiness to men, but right thinking and variety of thought.

43.

(99.) Repentance for base actions is the salvation of life.

45.

(48.) He who commits a wrong is more miserable than he who is wronged.

53.

(122.) Many who have learned no wisdom nevertheless live wisely.

60.

(114.) It is better to destroy one's own errors than those of others.

62.

(38.) It is good not only not to be unjust but not even to wish to be unjust.

64.

(190.) Many who have much knowledge have no understanding.

68.

(40.) The honourable man and the dishonourable are known not only from their actions but from their desires.

72.

(58.) Excessive longings for any object blind the soul to other things.

76.

(32.) Not words but misfortune is the teacher of the foolish.

83.

(28.) The cause of error is ignorance of the better.

98.

(211.) The friendship of one who has understanding is better than that of all who lack understanding

99.

(209.) He who possesses not a single good friend is not worthy to live.

102.

(51.) In all things the equal is fair, excess and defect displease me.

107.

(213.) Not all kinsmen are friends, but those who think alike about the common interest.

108.

(27.) Those who seek the good find it with difficulty; the evil they find even when they do not seek it.

117.

(ix. 72.) In reality we know nothing, for the truth lies in the depths.

THUCYDIDES

460–400 B.C.

The first historian in the modern sense, and at least one of the greatest. An Athenian general during the Peloponnesian war, he was banished for twenty years on account of failure in one expedition. His history of the war presents it as a conflict of opposing ideals, political and ethical, as well as of opposing kinds of force, naval and military. The typical Spartan character of endurance, reserve, silent strength, obedience to law, unquestioning devotion to the state, was admired by some of the greatest Athenians, especially Plato, whose ideal seems to have been a blending of this with the more liberal, cultured, humane Athenian type.

THE PRACTICAL IDEAL OF ATHENS

From the Funeral Oration of Pericles

THUCYDIDES ii. 37 *sq.* Greek Text: Bekker. The following translation is by Thomas Hobbes, 1588–1679.

We live not only free in the administration of the state but also one with another, void of jealousy touching each other's daily course of life; not offended at any man for following his own humour, nor casting on any man censorious looks, which though they be no punishment yet they grieve. So that conversing one with another in private without offence, we stand chiefly in fear to transgress against the public, and are obedient always to those that govern, and to the Laws, and principally to such laws as are written for protection against injury, and such unwritten as bring undeniable shame to the transgressors. We have also found out many ways to give our minds recreation from labour, by public institution of games, and sacrifices, for all the days of the year, and in the grace with which our private

F   39

life is ordered, by the daily delight whereof we expel sadness. We have this further by the greatness of our City, that all things from all parts of the earth are imported hither whereby we no less familiarly enjoy the products of other nations than our own.

39.

Then in the studies of war we excel our enemies in this, we leave our city open to all men; nor was it ever seen that by banishing of strangers we denied them the learning or right of any of those things by which if not hidden an enemy might reap advantage, not relying upon secret preparation and deceit but upon our own courage in the action. They in their discipline hunt after valour presently from their youth with laborious exercise, and we that live a more leisured life undertake as great danger as they.

(In these respects and in others our City is worthy of admiration.)

40.

For we are lovers of beauty without extravagance, and lovers of philosophy without indolence. We use riches rather for opportunities of action than for verbal ostentation, and hold it not a shame to confess poverty, but not to have avoided it. Moreover, there is in the same men a care both of their own and the public affairs, and a sufficient knowledge of state matters even in those that labour with their hands.

For we only think one that is utterly ignorant therein to be a man not that meddles with nothing, but that is good for nothing. We ourselves either make decisions or at least are zealous to understand our affairs, not accounting words a hindrance to action, but that it is rather a hindrance to action to come to it without instruction by discussion before. For also in this we excel others, daring to undertake as much as any, and yet examining what we undertake, whereas

with other men ignorance makes them dare, and consideration dastards. And they are most rightly reputed valiant who
though they perfectly apprehend both what is dangerous and
what is easy are never the more thereby diverted from adven-
turing. Again we are contrary to most men in bounty, for
we purchase our friends not by receiving but by bestowing
benefits.

In sum it may be said that our whole city is the school
of Greece, and that our citizens seem to me, each individually, able to present themselves for the greatest diversity of
action with grace and readiness.

The Spartan Character

From the speech of King Archidamus, THUCYDIDES i. 84.

As for the slackness and procrastination wherewith we
are reproached most of all, be never ashamed of it. For the
more haste you make to the war, the longer will you be before
you end it for that you go to it unprovided. Besides our city
hath ever been free and well thought of. And this to which
they object is rather to be called a modesty proceeding upon
judgment, for by that it is that we alone are neither arrogant
upon good success, nor shrink so much as others in adversity.
Nor are we when men provoke us to it with praise, through
the delight thereof, moved to undergo danger more than we
think fit ourselves. Nor when they sharpen us with repre-
hension doth the smart thereof a jot the more prevail upon
us. And this modesty of ours makes us both good soldiers
and good counsellors; good soldiers because shame is the
greater part of modesty and valour is most sensible of shame,
good counsellors in this that we are brought up more simply
than to disesteem the laws, and by severity more modest
than to disobey them. And also that we do not, like men

exceedingly wise in things needless, find fault bravely with
the preparation of the enemy and in effect not assault him
accordingly, but do think our neighbours' cogitations like
our own, and that the events of fortune cannot be discerned
by a speech, and do therefore always so furnish ourselves
really against the enemy as against men well advised. For
we ought not to build our hopes on their oversights, but upon
the safe foresight of ourselves. Nor must we think that
there is much difference between man and man, but him
only to be best who has been brought up amongst the
greatest difficulties. Let us not, therefore, cast aside the
institutions of our ancestors which we have so long retained
to our profit. Let us not hastily resolve in so small a part of
one day on what concerns many men's lives, much money,
many cities and much honour, but at leisure, the which we
have better commodity than any other to do, on account
of our power.

The Athenian and Spartan Types contrasted

From the speech of the Corinthian envoys, THUCYDIDES i. 70.

Besides, if there be any that may challenge to make
accusations against his neighbour, we think ourselves have
the right to do it, especially in such great quarrels as these.
Of these you neither seem to have any perception, nor
to consider what manner of men and how different from you
in every respect the Athenians be, that you are to contend
withal. For they love innovation and are swift to devise and
also to execute what they resolve on: but you on the contrary are only apt to save your own, not devise anything new,
nor scarce to attain what is necessary. They again are bold
beyond their strength, adventurous above their own reason,
and in danger hope still the best; whereas your actions are
ever beneath your power, and you distrust even what your

judgment assures and being in a danger never think to be delivered. They never pause, whilst you procrastinate; they love to be abroad, you at home most of any. For they make account of being abroad to add to their estate, you if you should go forth would think to impair your own. They, when they are victorious over their enemies advance the farthest, and when they are overcome by their enemies fall off the least. As for their bodies they use them in the service of the commonwealth as though they were none of their own, but their minds, when they would serve the state, are right their own. Unless they take in hand what they have once advised on, they account so much lost of their own. And when they take it in hand, if they obtain anything they think lightly of it in respect of what they expect to win by their prosecution. If they fail in any attempt they fill up the lack by forming fresh hopes. For they alone both hope for at once and have whatever they conceive, through their celerity in execution of what they once resolve on. And in this manner they labour and toil all the days of their lives, what they have they have no leisure to enjoy for continual getting of more. Nor holiday esteem they any than to do their duty, nor think they ease with nothing to do a less torment than laborious business, so that in a word to say they are men born neither to rest themselves nor suffer others is to say the truth.

On Revolutions. The effect of Political Disorder on Morals.

THUCYDIDES iii. 81. Thucydides' reflections upon revolutions seem to express the foreboding with which the most thoughtful of the Greeks foresaw the danger of the destruction of that creation of cultured social life they so highly prized through the restlessly contentious spirit of the race, and are applicable to all times of civil upheaval.

And many and heinous things happened in the cities through this sedition, which though they have been before and shall be ever as long as human nature is the same, yet are they greater or milder, and of different kinds, according to the several conjunctures of circumstance. For in peace and prosperity, as well cities as private men are better minded because they are not plunged into the necessity of acting against their will. But war taking away the affluence of daily necessaries is a most violent master and conformeth most men's passions to the present occasion.

(Thucydides describes how the customary meanings of words were changed, unreasoning audacity regarded as brave loyalty to party, moderation as cowardice, he who refused to plot a dissolver of his party. "To be revenged more in request than never to have received injury," the party tie stronger than the tie of blood, pledges broken by everyone who dared.)

The cause of all this is desire to rule, out of avarice and ambition, and the zeal of contention from those two proceeding. For such as were in authority in the cities, both of the one and the other faction, preferring under decent titles, the one the political equality of the multitude, the other the moderate aristocracy, though in words they seemed to be servants of the public, they made it in effect but the prize of their contention. And striving by whatever means to overcome, both ventured on most horrible outrages and prosecuted their revenges still further, without any regard of justice or the public good, but limiting them, each faction by their own appetites, and stood ready, whether by unjust sentence or having seized the power, by their own force to satisfy their present spite. So that whilst neither had any regard for piety, those who succeeded in carrying through a hateful act under a plausible pretext were more commended. The neutrals among the citizens were destroyed by both factions, partly because they would not side with them and partly for envy that they should so escape.

83.

Thus was wickedness of every kind on foot throughout

Greece, by the occasion of their sedition. Simplicity, whereof there is much in a generous nature, was laughed down. And it was far the best course to stand dissidently against each other with their thoughts in battle array.

The common course of life being at that time compounded in the city, the nature of man which is wont even against law to do evil, gotten now above the Law, showed itself with delight to be too weak for passion, too strong for justice and enemy to all superiority. For else they would never have preferred revenge to what is sacred, nor lucre before justice.

THOMAS HOBBES.

XENOPHON'S "MEMORABILIA"

Socrates (470–399 B.C.) wrote nothing himself, but devoted his life to arousing his fellow-citizens, individually, especially the young, to serious thought about life, and to the recognition that self-knowledge is the precondition of all useful activity. His effect upon them is described in Plato's *Dialogues* as analogous to the electric shock of the torpedo-fish. According to Aristotle, we owe to Socrates the beginnings of logic and of ethical enquiry. How far Plato's Socrates is the real Socrates is a problem which will never be solved. The immense personal effect he had upon Plato must have been due to great philosophic as well as moral power. By Plato Socrates seems to have been regarded as the spirit of philosophy itself, always searching, and serving truth alone, in thought and life, always rejoicing if his fellow-workers can show him a better way. Xenophon presents to us only a part portrait of such a man, but not inconsistent in the main features.

The following passages will illustrate the method of Socrates, so far as it was appreciated by Xenophon.

In the *Memorabilia* Xenophon aimed at presenting Socrates' way of life and discourses in such a way as to disprove the charges that he was irreligious and a corrupter of youth, on which he was condemned to death.

Self-knowledge

MEMORABILIA Bk. III. ch. vii. sect. 1. The text is that of the Rev. Percival Frost (nearly corresponding with Kühner's).

Observing that Charmides, the son of Glaucon, was a man of remarkable gifts, and much more able than those who were at that time exercising political power, but hesitating to come before the people and take a part in public affairs, Socrates said to him:

" Tell me, Charmides—What sort of man would you deem him to be who though capable of winning the wreath of victory in the great contests, and through this gaining honour for himself and greater fame for his fatherland in Greece, should be unwilling to compete? "

46

"Obviously," he replied, "a poor-spirited and craven fellow."

"And if," continued Socrates, "anyone capable of conducting the affairs of the city and increasing its prosperity, and thus winning esteem for himself, should be reluctant to do this, would it not be reasonable to describe him as weak-spirited?"

"Perhaps," he said; "but what is your object in asking me this?"

"Because," said Socrates, "I consider that you have this capacity, and are hesitating to exercise it, and that too in matters in which it is essential that you should take part, since you are a citizen."

"In what kind of pursuits," said Charmides, "have you observed this capacity of mine, so as to have discovered that I have it?"

"In social meetings," he replied, "in which you are present with those engaged in politics, for whenever they consult you in anything, I notice that you give good counsel, and that when they are in error your corrections are just."

"It is not the same thing," he said, "Socrates, to discuss in private and to take part in public controversy."

"And yet," observed Socrates, "he who is able to reckon does not reckon less when in a large company than in solitude, and those who play the flute best in solitary places excel also before the multitude."

"Do you not see," said Charmides, "that shame and fear are innate in men, and are round about them much more in crowds than in private gatherings?"

"I am bent," returned Socrates, "on showing you that although you are not too bashful before the wisest or timid before the strongest, you are ashamed to speak before the most foolish and weak. Is it before the cloth-carders that you are ashamed, or the cobblers, or the carpenters, or the coppersmiths, or the husbandmen, or those who barter goods in the market-place and are intent on the question what they can buy for less and sell for more? For it is of all these that the assembly consists. How do you suppose does your conduct differ from that of a strong man well trained who is afraid of the non-professionals? For you would not otherwise, seeing that you are able to converse easily with the first men in the city, some of whom think little of you, and since you are also greatly superior to those whose business it is to speak in public, hesitate to address persons who have given no thought to political affairs, nor have any contempt for you, from fear of ridicule."

" What," said Charmides, " do you not think that the members of the assembly often laugh at people who are speaking well? "

" And so do your other associates," he said, " and I am therefore astonished that whilst you readily submit when they do this, you suppose that you will be utterly unable to endure the others. Beware, my dear friend, of self-ignorance, and do not make the mistake which the majority make. For the majority, eager to look into the affairs of others, do not give their attention to self-examination. Do not, then, be neglectful of this, but rather strive to give heed to yourself. Neither be negligent of what concerns the city, if in any matter it may prosper better through you. For when the interests of the state are best maintained, not only will the other citizens, but also your friends and you yourself not least, reap the advantage."

Wisdom and Virtue

MEMORABILIA Bk. III. ch. ix. sec. 1.

On another occasion Socrates was asked whether courage can be taught, or comes by nature. " I think," he said,

" that just as one body is by nature stronger for labour than another, so also one soul is by nature more robust than another in relation to objects of fear. For I notice that persons reared in the same regulations and practices differ greatly amongst themselves in daring. I am of opinion, however, that every kind of nature may grow in courage through training and discipline. For it is obvious that the Scythians and the Thracians would not dare to fight against the Lacedaemonians armed with shields and spears, and evident also that neither would the Lacedaemonians be willing to have a contest with the Thracians arrayed in light shields with darts, nor the Scythians with bows. Equally in all other cases I observe that men both differ by nature from each other and also advance much through training.

" Hence it is evident that all alike, both those who are naturally gifted and those who are more dull by nature, ought both to study and to practise in those matters in which they desire to excel."

Between wisdom and temperance he did not distinguish, but he judged to be wise and temperate the man who knows what is noble and right so as to practise it, and perceives what is base so as to beware of it. When further questioned whether he would hold wise and self-controlled those who know what they ought to do, but do the opposite—"No more do I hold them so," he said, "than unwise and incontinent. For all, I think, choosing out of the possibilities presented to them what they suppose to be most beneficial to themselves, act accordingly. I consider, therefore, those who do not act rightly to be neither wise nor temperate." He said, also, that justice and every other virtue is wisdom. "For just acts, and all acts that are done virtuously, are beautiful and worthy. And neither those who know these could prefer anything else to them, nor are those who do not know them capable of performing them, and even if they make the attempt, they fail. Thus the wise do acts which are both beautiful and good, those who are not wise are not able for these acts, and if they try, they fail. Since, therefore, just acts and all others that are noble and worthy are performed through virtue, it is evident that justice and every other virtue is wisdom."

Madness he said to be the opposite of wisdom, but he did not call lack of science madness. Nearest to madness he considered ignorance of self to be, and to have beliefs about what one does not know, and to suppose oneself to have knowledge. But the majority, as he said, do not hold those who are in error in matters of which most are ignorant to be mad, rather they call mad those who are in error in matters of which the majority have knowledge. If anyone should suppose himself to be so great as to make the gates of the fort incline as he passed through, or so strong as to try to lift up a house, or to make any of those attempts the impossibility of which is evident to all, this they say to be madness. Those who err a little are not thought by the multitude to be mad, but just as they call a great desire love, so they call a great folly madness.

.   .   .   .   .   .

Virtue is Knowledge

Memorabilia Bk. III. ch. ix. sec. 10.

"Kings and rulers," he said, "are not those who hold the sceptre, nor those elected by the men in the street, nor those on whom the lot falls, nor those who exercise force or fraud, but those who know how to rule." When it had been granted that it is the part of the ruler to direct what should be done, and of the subject to obey, he would point out that on shipboard it is the man of knowledge—that is, the captain—who rules, and all the others in the ship obey him who knows, and in agriculture the owners of land, in illness those who understand sickness, in athletics those in training. And so with all whose affairs are in need of management, if they suppose themselves to possess the knowledge for this purpose, well and good, but otherwise they not only follow those who know if they are on the spot, but send for them if absent so that in obeying these persons they may do right. Again he showed that in wool-spinning the women direct the men, for the reason that they know how to spin and the men do not.

And if anyone should object to this that the tyrant can refuse obedience to those who know best—"How then," he said, "would it be possible to disobey, when there is a penalty imposed upon anyone who refuses to follow good counsel? For he will go wrong, and the man who goes wrong will be punished." And if one were to observe that the tyrant has power to slay the high-minded man—"Do you suppose," Socrates would say, "the man who puts to death the strongest of his allies to be unpunished, or to be only slightly harmed? Or whether do you think that one who acts thus would be more likely to be preserved or to be destroyed in the very quickest way possible?"

When someone asked him what he thought to be the most excellent way of life for a man, he answered, "Well-doing."

Asked again whether he considered good fortune to be a way of life, "I hold," he said, "fortune and practice to be altogether opposed. Good fortune I think to be the attainment of anything that is advantageous without seeking for it. Right practice I hold to be the study and discipline in well-doing, and those who devote themselves to this seem to me to practise aright. The best and dearest to God," he added, "are those who do well in husbandry the duties of husbandry, in medicine the duties belonging to medicine, in statesmanship political duties, but the man who does nothing well is neither useful nor dear to God."

PLATO

427–347 B.C.

Was born and died in Athens. He was a pupil of Socrates, 408–399 B.C., founded the Academy, 387–6 B.C., visited Sicily three times, and endeavoured without success to influence Dionysius II. ethically and politically.

Plato's moral philosophy is essentially bound up with his philosophy of the universe, although from many of his *Dialogues* a clear conception of his moral ideal and ethical teaching can be gathered, without development of the metaphysical background. He illustrates in the highest degree that union of the mystical and scientific genius which some have thought essential to the philosopher.

Crito and Socrates in Prison

CRITO. Greek Text: C. F. Hermann. Crito, one of Socrates' friends, visits him in prison and endeavours to persuade him to escape, for which object ample resources have been provided by Socrates' friends.

Crito. But, O Socrates, best of friends, even at this hour be persuaded by me and save yourself. For if you should die, not one misfortune alone would befall me, but in addition to my being bereaved of such a friend as I shall never find again, many who do not know us well, will suppose that though I could have saved you, if I had been willing to spend money, I failed to do so. And what more shameful reputation could there be than this, to value money more than one's friends! For most people will not be persuaded that you have refused to escape in spite of our entreaties.

Socrates. But why, dear Crito, does the opinion of the multitude matter so much to us? For the righteous, whom we ought to regard more, will think that these things have happened as they have happened.

Crito. But you see none the less, Socrates, that it is necessary to take heed also of the opinion of the multitude. This very thing is evident from the present circumstances, that they are able to bring about not the least of evils, but almost the greatest, when anyone has been calumniated before them.

Socrates. Would indeed, Crito, that the multitude were able to cause the greatest evils, if thereby they were able also to cause the greatest good! Fortunate would that be! As it is, they are capable of neither. For they are able to make a man neither wise nor unwise, but they do whatever chance suggests to them.

Crito. Be that as it may. But tell me this, Socrates, whether it is that you are concerned for me and our other friends, presuming that if you escape from here the informers will make things unpleasant for us, as having let you get away secretly, and we shall be compelled either to spend all our substance—or much of it—or to suffer some other trouble? If you have any fear of this kind, you may dismiss it. For it is right that in rescuing you we should run not only this danger but a greater than this. Nay, listen to me and do not deny me.

Socrates. I do consider these things, Crito, and much besides.

Crito. Do not then fear anything of the kind. For those who are willing to save you, and take you hence, do not want much money. And further, do you not see how easily bought these informers are, and not much money is needed for them?

.   .   .   .   .   .

Neither let it be grievous to you, as you said at the trial, that if you should leave this city you would not know what use to make of your life. For in all parts people will welcome you, wherever you may go. But if you should be willing to go to Thessaly, I have friends there who would greatly regard you, and ensure your safety, so that no one should molest you in Thessaly. Moreover, Socrates, you do not seem to me to be doing what is right in abandoning yourself, when you can save yourself, and being in haste to bring upon yourself the very same thing which enemies might strive and have striven to compass, aiming at your destruction. Further, you appear to me to betray those whom it lies in you to bring up and educate, when you abandon them altogether and depart, so that, as far as you are concerned, their doings are left to chance. And as is probable, they will meet with the lot which usually falls to the share of orphans. For we ought either not to give birth to children or to share their fortunes, both bringing them up and educating them. But you seem to choose the easier part. You ought, however, to choose the part which a good and brave man would choose, you who profess to have cultivated virtue throughout life. I am ashamed therefore, both on your account and for ourselves your friends, lest this whole drama of which you are the hero should seem to have taken place through a sort of cowardice on our part, both the entrance of the accusation, as it were, into the court of justice, when it was introduced, though it need not have been introduced, and the manner of the process of the trial itself, and now the final act, the tragi-comic *dénouement*, in which we appear through meanness and cowardice to have got off, not saving you, who will not save yourself though it was possible, and practicable if there were even a little resource in us. Look then, Socrates, whether these things are not base and dishonourable, both to you and to us. Nay, do bethink yourself. Indeed it is no longer the hour to think of resolving, but to have resolved. There is only one counsel. For on the coming night the whole thing must be carried through. If we delay at all it is impossible and no longer open to us. Wherefore on every account, Socrates, be persuaded and do not say me nay.

Socrates. Dear Crito, your ardour on my behalf is a

precious thing if it accords with duty, but if not, then the
more pressing it is so much the more is it dangerous. We must
therefore now consider whether this ought to be done or
not. For I am now, as I have always been, incapable of persuasion by anything in myself but the principle which my
reason shows me to be the best. Principles which I have in
past times maintained I cannot now, when this fate has come
upon me, cast aside, but they seem to me exactly the same,
and I reverence and honour them as the same, even as before.
If then we have none better to substitute for these, know well
that I shall not yield to you, even though the power of the
multitude could terrify us as if we were children, bringing to
bear more horrors in the shape of chains and deaths, and
confiscations. What then will be the most fitting method of
enquiring into this question? Shall we first take up again
the argument you brought forward in regard to opinions,
considering whether or not it was a sound position that we
ought under all conditions to give weight to some opinions
and not to others? Or shall we hold that it was indeed a
sound position before I was condemned to die, but that now
it is evident that it was idly said for the sake of argument,
whilst in reality it was a joke, a kind of banter? This is what
I want to examine, together with you, Crito, whether the
principle appears to have changed now that I am in my
present situation, or whether it remains the same, and whether
we shall abandon it or conform to it. As I hold, it has
always been the view of people who weigh their words,
as it is my view now, that of human opinions we ought to
value some highly, others not at all. By all that is sacred,
Crito, does not this seem true to you? For you, humanly
speaking, are in no danger of dying to-morrow, and the
present mischance need not confuse your judgment. Reflect,
therefore, does it not seem to you a good saying that not all
human opinions ought we to honour, but to honour some

G

and not others, nor all men's opinions, but those of some men, and of others not? What do you say? Am I not right in this?

Crito. You are.

Socrates. We should honour, then, the good opinions and not the bad?

Crito. Yes.

Socrates. Are not the good opinions those of the wise, the bad those of the foolish?

Crito. Who could deny it?

(By means of various illustrations, Socrates leads Crito to agree that in regard to right and wrong we need not care for the opinion of any except the man who understands what truth herself would say. And though the multitude may have power to kill, it is not mere living that is to be most valued, but living well, and living well means living nobly and rightly. These principles granted, Socrates passes by Crito's appeals as irrelevant and turning on questions which merely have interest for the majority, and invites him to join in the examination of the only question which ought to be considered, viz., whether it is right for him to escape, contrary to the decision of the Athenians.)

49.

Socrates. Are we to say that we ought under no circumstances to do wrong voluntarily, or that in certain circumstances we ought to do wrong, in others not? Or is it never either good or noble to do wrong, as we so often agreed in the past? Or on the contrary, have all these former agreements of ours been swept away in these few days and have we, Crito, all this long while at our time of life, when engaged in earnest discussion with one another, not realised that we were in no wise better than children? Or is it not rather in every way as we then agreed, whether or not the multitude think the same and whether more or less grievous sufferings are to befall us than the present, that notwithstanding all this, wrong-doing is in every respect both an evil and a base thing for the wrong-doer? Do we say thus or not?

Crito. We do say it.

Socrates. Under no conditions, then, must one do wrong?

Crito. Assuredly not.

Socrates. Neither when wronged ought one to wrong in return as the multitude suppose, since wrong should never be done?

Crito. It seems not.

Socrates. What then? Ought one to do an injury to anyone, Crito, or not?

Crito. I suppose not, Socrates.

Socrates. Well, then, to return evil for evil—is this just, as the many say, or unjust?

Crito. By no means just.

Socrates. One may not, then, render wrong for wrong, nor do harm to any man, whatever one may suffer at his hands. Take good heed, Crito, whether in conceding this you do not concede it against your own view, for know that few are they who believe this, and will believe it. And for those who do and those who do not hold this view there is no counsel in common, but they despise one another of necessity when they perceive each other's creeds. Give, therefore, very earnest consideration to this question, whether you are at one with me and share my views, and we may begin our deliberations from this standpoint—namely, that it is never right either to do wrong or to requite wrong with wrong, nor having suffered evil to defend oneself by doing evil in return. Or do you dissent at this point, not sharing this principle? As for me, both of old and still to-day this is what I believe. You, if you are of any other opinion, speak and declare it. But if you abide by the former principle, hear what follows from it.

Crito. But I do abide by it and accept it. Therefore say on.

Socrates. I will then declare what follows, or rather I

will put a question. Ought one to carry out a just undertaking to which he has agreed or avoid it by deception?

Crito. It should be carried out.

Socrates. This granted, consider the next point. If we
depart hence without the consent of the city, shall we be
wronging anyone, even those whom it least behoves us to
wrong, or shall we not, and shall we be standing firmly by
our just undertakings or not?

Crito. I hardly know, Socrates, how to answer your
questions. I do not understand.

Socrates. Well then, look at it in this way. If we proceed
to run away from here, or however else this ought to be
described, suppose that the laws and the commonwealth of
the state, presenting themselves before us, should ask, " Tell
us, O Socrates, what is it that you purpose to do? Do you
suppose that in this act which you are attempting you are
doing anything else but preparing the downfall of ourselves,
the laws, and the whole city, so far as it lies in you? Or
do you imagine that that city in which the established
decrees have no force but can be rendered invalid and of no
effect, can any longer exist and not be overturned?" What
are we to say, Crito, to these and similar complaints? For
much more might be said, especially by an orator, on behalf
of the principle thus endangered that the decisions of the
law courts must hold good. Or shall we reply to them that
the city has done us wrong, and not pronounced justly in
this judgment? Shall we say this, or what shall we say?

Crito. This, by the Gods, Socrates!

Socrates. What then if the laws should say, " O Socrates,
was this what was agreed between us and you, or was it
that you should abide by the judgment which the city might
pronounce?" And if we should be surprised at what they say,
perhaps they would continue, " O Socrates, marvel not at
what has been said, but give answer, since you are in the

habit of speaking by question and answer, what charge have you to bring against us and the state, for which you plot our destruction? Did we not in the first place bring you into being, and through us your father took your mother to wife and gave birth to you? Say then, do you complain of those laws amongst us in regard to marriage as defective? "

I have no complaint, I should say—" Or of those in which you were brought up which have to do with the rearing and education of the child? Or were the laws which relate to these matters requiring that your father should educate you in music and gymnastic not well laid down?" "Well," I should reply—" Well then, after you were born, brought up and educated can you in the first place deny that you were both our offspring and servant, both you and your parents? and if this is so, do you suppose that right is equal as between you and us and that it is just when we do anything against you that you should retaliate? Or is it the case that whereas you have no equal right in relation to your father, or your master, if you have one, such that you may retaliate what you have suffered or retort if corrected, or strike again if struck, or anything else of the kind?—in the case, on the other hand, of your fatherland and the laws, this is permissible, so that if we go about to destroy you, because we hold this to be right, you also so far as you are able will attempt to destroy in return the laws and the country, and will maintain that in doing this you do right, you a person who is really zealous for virtue? Or are you astute to the point of not knowing that your country is of higher value than your father and mother and all your ancestors, and more honourable and sacred and of greater importance, both before gods and before men possessed of understanding, and that one ought to reverence and yield to and cherish yet more an offended country than a father and either persuade or do whatever it commands, and if it lay suffering upon you, to suffer patiently, though this were to endure stripes or imprisonment? Or that if it send us to war, to be wounded or killed, this ought to be done and this is right, and that in no case must we give way nor retreat, nor abandon our post, but, alike in war and in the law-court and everywhere, either the commands of the state and the country must be carried out, or we are bound to convince the state wherein true justice consists. For it is not permitted to use force against either mother or father, much less against one's country." What shall we say to this, Crito? Do the laws say truly or not?

Crito. Truly as it seems to me.

Socrates. " Consider, therefore, O Socrates," the laws may perhaps say, " if we have spoken truth in this, that you are not right in making the attempt which you are now making. For we who have brought you into the world, reared and educated you, bestowing on you as on other citizens all the noble gifts of which we are capable, nevertheless through the freedom we have given to any Athenian who desires it, we proclaim to anyone who is not content with us after he has been examined for citizenship and has seen the administration of the city and ourselves the laws, that he is at liberty to take whatever is his own, and go away whithersoever he will.

" And none of us the laws stands in the way or forbids if any of you wish to go to a colony, or elsewhere, should ourselves and the city not please him, there to go wherever he will, taking his possessions. But whosoever amongst you remains, having seen after what manner we exercise justice, and in other respects administer the city, then we say that this man has agreed by his action that whatever we command that he will do. And the man who disobeys we declare to have committed a threefold wrong, inasmuch as in disobeying us he disobeys those who have given him life, and those who have brought him up, and inasmuch as having agreed to obey he neither obeys nor shows us convincingly in what we have done ill. And whereas instead of harshly commanding him to do what we ordered, we put before him and allowed him to choose one of two courses, either to convince us of injustice or to do our behests, he does neither of these.

"You also, O Socrates," we say, "lay yourself open to these charges if you carry out what you propose, you not less than any other Athenian, but rather more than all." And if I should ask, "wherefore?" perhaps they would with justice bring against me that, most of all the Athenians, I have entered into this agreement with them. For, they would say, "O Socrates, we have striking evidence that you are content both with us and the city. For you would not have made it your home in a more special way than all the other Athenians if it did not very specially content you.

.   .   .   .   .   .

"Even in this very trial it was open to you to pay the price of exile if you wished and then to do with the consent of the state what you now are planning without its consent. But you then affected not to find it grievous if you had to die, but to choose, as you said, death before exile. But now neither ashamed of those words, nor showing respect for us the laws, but plotting to destroy us, you act as the most contemptible slave might act, since you attempt to run away, contrary to contracts, and undertakings according to which you have agreed to live under our polity. First then make answer to us on this point: whether we say truly or not that you have agreed to live under our government, in deed, not merely in word?" What shall we say to this, O Crito? Can we do anything but agree?

Crito. Of necessity, Socrates.

Socrates. Is it not then true they would say that you are

transgressing your contracts and agreements with us, which you made not under compulsion, nor because you were deceived, nor forced to come to a decision in a short time, since you had seventy years in which it was possible for you to go away, if we did not satisfy you, and the compacts did not appear to you just? But you did not prefer Lacedaemon nor Crete, which you have ever spoken of as well-ordered states, neither any other of the Greek cities, nor the barbarian, but have been less away than the lame, the blind, and other incapables. So striking beyond that of the other Athenians is your satisfaction with the city and evidently with ourselves the laws. For the city would delight no one without laws. And now will you not abide by your undertakings? You will, if you will follow us, O Socrates, and you will not make yourself ridiculous by escaping from the city. Think further of this—what good will you effect for yourself and your friends, if you transgress and do this wrong? For that your friends will themselves run the risk of being exiled and deprived of the state or of losing their substance is almost certain. As for yourself, in the first place if you should go to one of the cities in the immediate neighbourhood— Thebes or Megara, for both are well-governed—you will come in the guise of an enemy, Socrates, to their constitution, and those who cherish their own states will look with suspicion on you as a destroyer of the laws, and you will confirm the opinion of the judges, so that they will seem to have given a just verdict. For he who is a destroyer of the laws will *a fortiori* be regarded as a corrupter of youth and of simple people. But perchance you will avoid the well-ordered and most law-abiding cities. And if you do this, will life then be of any value to you? Or will you betake yourself to these and converse with them without shame—on what themes, O Socrates? Will the tenor of your discourse be, as here, that virtue and justice are of the highest value to men and what is lawful, and the laws, and do you not think that the doings of Socrates would then appear shameful?

. . . . . .

But, O Socrates, be persuaded by us who brought you up, and do not value either children or life or anything else whatever more than duty, so that when you go to the other world you may have all this for your defence before those who rule there, for neither here does it seem better, juster, or more holy to do this either for you or for any of those dear to you, neither when you arrive thither will it be better. Now, indeed, you depart, if you depart, having suffered a wrong, not from us the laws, but from men. But if you escape, thus basely paying wrong with wrong, and rendering evil for evil, transgressing your agreements and compacts with us, and injuring those whom it least befits you to injure, yourself, your friends, your country, and ourselves, we shall be displeased with you during your life, and our brothers there the laws in the other world will not receive you with friendliness, knowing that you have tried, so far as in you lay, to destroy us.

Know, O dear friend Crito, that I seem to hear these things as the mystics hear the flutes, and in me the sound of these words murmurs and renders me deaf to all other sounds. But know that, as it now seems to me, if you speak against these words you will speak in vain. Nevertheless, if you think you can thereby do more, say on.

Crito. But, O Socrates, I have nothing to say.

Socrates. Then, Crito, let us do thus, since thus God leads.

The Nature of the Soul, and its longing to be free from the distracting influence of the Body

PHAEDO xxvi. 79. Greek Text: Archer-Hind's Edition. The longer passage in illustration of this principle, and the true life of the philosopher as a life of the spirit, is given in Mr. Cornford's volume (*Greek Religion*). The following will illustrate here this important line of thought in Plato, leading at times to a greater dualism and asceticism than belongs to his philosophy universally.

Socrates. Shall we declare that there are two kinds of existence, the one visible, the other invisible?

Cebes. Let us do so.

Socrates. And that the unseen are eternally the same, but the visible never the same, ever changing?

Cebes. This also let us grant.

Socrates. Well then, in our own case, is not one part of us body, the other soul?

Cebes. Certainly.

Socrates. To which then is our body more like in its form, and more akin?

Cebes. It must be evident to everyone that it resembles more the visible.

Socrates. How is it with the soul, is it visible or invisible?

Cebes. To men, at least, it is not visible, Socrates.

Socrates. But, of course, when we speak of visible and invisible, we speak of the nature of man. Or are you thinking of any other?

Cebes. No, but of the human.

Socrates. What then are we to say of the soul, that it is visible or not visible?

Cebes. Not visible.

Socrates. The soul then is more like the unseen, the body like the visible?

Cebes. Necessarily so, Socrates.

Socrates. And did we not say before that the soul, whenever it makes use of the body in order to consider anything, whether by means of sight or hearing, or any other sense— for this is equivalent to use of the body, when we perceive through one of the senses—is then drawn by the body towards that which is never the same, and wanders, loses her way, is confused, and is seized with giddiness, as though drunk, for such are the things that she grasps?

Cebes. Certainly.

Socrates. But when on the other hand she is engaged in thought by herself, she passes to that which is pure and eternal, and immortal, and immutable, and as she is akin to this, she cleaves ever to it when she belongs to herself, and is capable of it. Then has she rest from her wanderings, and in dwelling with these is ever the same, seeing that the things she grasps are constant, and this state of hers is called wisdom.

Cebes. Nobly and truly do you speak in every way, Socrates.

Socrates. To which then of those two forms does the soul seem to you more similar and akin according to our previous consideration and the present?

Cebes. Everyone, as it seems to me, Socrates, even the slowest of understanding, will agree on this method that the soul is altogether and in every way more like to the eternal than to the changing.

Socrates. And the body?

Cebes. More to that which changes.

Socrates. Consider the matter also in this way When the soul and the body are together, nature directs the one to serve and obey, the other to rule and command. Here also which appears to resemble the divine, and which the mortal? Do you not think that it befits the divine to rule and lead, the mortal to be ruled and to serve?

Cebes. I do.

Socrates. Which then does the soul resemble?

Cebes. Clearly, Socrates, the soul is like the divine, the body the mortal.

Socrates. Consider then, Cebes, whether from all that has been said the soul is most like to that which is divine, immortal, and intelligible, simple, indissoluble, and ever the same, and identical with itself, whilst the body again is like the human and object of sense, and composite, and dissoluble, and never the same with itself. Or have we anything else to say, O dear Cebes, against this?

Cebes. We have not.

Socrates. Well then, since this is so, is not the body such as to be quickly dissolved, the soul on the other hand such as to be quite indissoluble or very nearly so?

Cebes. How should it be otherwise?

.   .   .   .   .   .

(The body, however, especially if embalmed, may last a great number of years.)

Socrates. And the soul, that invisible being, departs to a region like unto itself, noble, pure and invisible, that is to the world beyond, in reality to the good and allwise God, whither, if God will, my soul also must presently depart. Shall this, a being of this nature and endowment, when released from the body, be as the majority believe, straightway dispersed and destroyed?

Far from it, dear Cebes and Simmias, much rather is this the truth. If the soul is pure when released, dragging with her no stain of the body, seeing that she did not willingly share aught with it during life, but fled from it and remained withdrawn unto herself, inasmuch as she is ever practising this, this is nothing else but to be truly philosophising, and in reality preparing for death? Is this anything but the preparation for death?

Cebes. Certainly it is this.

Socrates. If then, in this condition, the soul departs, to that which is like herself, the invisible, divine, immortal, wise, there arriving she has felicity, delivered from wandering, and ignorance, and fears, and wild passions, and all other human evils, and as is said by the initiated, passing in truth the remaining time with the gods. Shall we say thus, Cebes, or otherwise?

Cebes. Thus indeed, by Heaven.

Prayer of Socrates

PHAEDRUS 279. Greek Text: C. F. Hermann.

O beloved Pan and the other Gods who dwell here, grant to me that I be beautiful within, and that all I have of external things be in harmony with that which is inward. May I deem only the wise to be rich, and may my possessions be such as no other than the right-minded would bear or hold.

Better to be wronged than to wrong

GORGIAS 466a. Greek Text: C. F. Hermann. *Cf.* also edition of Gonzalez Lodge (College Series of Greek Authors, U.S.A.). Socrates wishes to know from Gorgias (of Leontini), the famous sophist and orator, what is his own conception of his art, and its value to the world. Gorgias hands over the discussion to one of his pupils, Polus. Later Callicles, a man of the world with political interests, unable to endure what seems to him to be Socrates' unpractical treatment of the argument, enters the lists.

Socrates develops the original issue into the question of happiness, whether it belongs more to prosperous injustice or justice in the greatest misfortune. Callicles maintains the doctrine that might is right, according to the law of Nature.

Polus. What then, do you suppose that distinguished orators are regarded as flatterers and thought of with contempt in our cities?

Socrates. They are not thought of at all, in my opinion.

Polus. How? Not thought of? Do they not possess the greatest power in cities?

Socrates. Not so, if by possession of power you mean possession of something which is good for the possessor.

Polus. Certainly I mean that.

Socrates. To me then it appears that of all citizens orators have the least power.

Polus. What do you mean? Are they not able like tyrants to slay at their desire, and deprive of their possessions, and expel from cities whomsoever they choose to expel?

Socrates. By Heaven! Polus, I am in doubt, at every word you say, whether you speak as yourself and reveal your own mind, or put the question to me.

Polus. Why, I am questioning you.

Socrates. Well then, my friend, why do you ask me two questions at the same time?

Polus. How two?

Socrates. Did you not just now say something of this kind, that orators put to death whomsoever they will, like tyrants, and deprive them of their possessions, and banish from cities as seems good to them?

Polus. Certainly I did.

Socrates. I tell you then that these are two questions. I shall therefore give you two answers. For I say, Polus, even as I said before, that orators and tyrants have less power than anyone in cities. For they do not realise any of the objects they desire, so to speak. Nevertheless they do what seems best to themselves.

Polus. Is not this to have great power?

Socrates. Not so, according to Polus.

Polus. But according to me it is—I say they have.

Socrates. By Heaven, you don't!—since you say that to have great power is a good to him who has it.

Polus. Of course I do.

Socrates. Do you then hold it to be a good when a man out of his mind does what seems best to him, and do you call this having great power?

Polus. No, I don't.

Socrates. Are you going to confute me by proving that orators are in their senses and possessed of an art of rhetoric and not of flattery? If you leave me unrefuted, then neither those orators who do whatever seems good to them in cities, nor the tyrants, have any real good in this capacity of theirs. But power is, as you say, a good, whilst the senseless doing of what seems good even you agree to be an evil. Isn't it so?

Polus. I agree.

Socrates. How then are the orators or the tyrants able to do great things in cities, if Socrates is not confuted through a demonstration of Polus that they do what they will to do?

Polus. What does the man mean?

Socrates. I say that they do not effect what they desire —well then, confute me.

Polus. Did you not lately—just before this—admit that they do what seems best to them?

Socrates. Yes—and I admit it still.

Polus. And do they not bring about what they want?

Socrates. That I do not allow.

Polus. Though they do what seems to them best?

Socrates. Even so.

Polus. What you are saying, Socrates, is intolerable and monstrous.

Socrates. Do not scold, good Polus (I address you in your own style); but if you have any question to put to me, show that I speak falsely—if not, answer yourself.

Polus. Well then, I am willing to answer, in order to find out what you mean.

Socrates. Whether then do you suppose that men desire the performance of the acts they happen to be doing, or rather desire that object for the sake of which they do what they are doing? For example, take the case of persons drinking medicine prescribed by doctors. Do you suppose the object of their desires to be what they are actually doing— namely taking medicine, and suffering for it—or is their object health?

Polus. Obviously the object is health.

Socrates. Again, those who engage in ocean trade, or transact any other business, are not in all their transactions doing what they desire; for who would want to go to sea, running risks and taking much trouble? But they aim at that, I suppose, on account of which they put to sea, namely, to be rich; for they sail for the sake of wealth.

Polus. Certainly.

Socrates. Is it not then the same in all cases—if anyone does something as a means, he does not want that which he does, but the end, for the sake of which he does it?

Polus. Yes.

Socrates. Are there then certain things which are neither good nor evil, but lying between these not good and not bad?

Polus, Necessarily so, Socrates.

Socrates. Would you then say that wisdom and health and riches and other things of this kind are good, their opposite evil?

Polus. I would.

Socrates. By things neither good nor evil, I suppose you would mean those which sometimes partake of good, sometimes of evil, sometimes of neither, such as sitting and walking and running and sailing, and again stones and wood, and other such things? Is this not what you mean? Or is it something else which you call neither good nor evil?

Polus. No, it is these.

Socrates. Do people, then, do the things which are indifferent for the sake of the good things, or the good for the sake of these?

Polus. Presumably the things indifferent for the sake of the good.

Socrates. It is then in the pursuit of the good that we walk, whenever we do so, because we suppose this to be better, and again, stand still, for the same object, the good— is it not?

Polus. Yes.

Socrates. Accordingly when we put anyone to death, and banish or take away his possessions, we do so because we suppose it to be better for us to do these things than not to do them?

Polus. Most assuredly.

Socrates. Those then who do these things do them all for the sake of the good?

Polus. So I say.

Socrates. We are agreed then that when we do aught as a means to something, we do not desire our action itself, but that end for which we act.

Polus. Doubtless.

Socrates. We do not then desire to slay, nor banish from our cities, nor take anyone's possessions absolutely, but we desire to do these things if they happen to be beneficial; if injurious, we do not desire them. For we desire what is good, as you say, but we do not desire what is neither good nor evil, nor what is evil. Is it not so? Do I seem to you to speak the truth, Polus, or not? Why do you not answer?

Polus. You speak truth.

Socrates. Accordingly, since we are so far agreed—If a man puts anyone to death or banishes or deprives him of his possessions, whether he be tyrant or orator, supposing what he does to be better for himself, whereas it happens to be worse, this man presumably does what seems good to him?

H

Polus. Yes.

Socrates. Well, does he also what he desires if these things happen to be evil? Why do you not answer?

Polus. Well then, he does not seem to me to do what he desires.

Socrates. Can it be, then, that such an one has great power in this city, if to have great power is, according to your admission, a good?

Polus. It cannot.

Socrates. I spoke then truly when I said that it is possible for a man though doing in his city what seems good to him not to have great power, nor to do what he desires?

Polus. As if you, Socrates, would not accept the chance of being able to do what seems good to you in the city, rather than not, and would not be envious when you see anyone slaying whom he liked, or taking his possessions, or putting him in prison!

Socrates. Justly, do you mean, or unjustly?

Polus. Howsoever he might do it, would he not be enviable in both cases?

Socrates. Have a care what you say, O Polus.

Polus. Why so?

Socrates. Because we ought not to envy the unenviable, nor the miserable, but to pity them.

Polus. What? Does this seem to you to be the state of those men of whom I speak?

Socrates. How otherwise?

Polus. Does, then, one who puts to death as seems good to him, justly doing so, seem to you miserable and pitiable?

Socrates. Not so—yet not enviable.

Polus. Did you not just now say that he was miserable?

Socrates. If he slays unjustly, my friend, and pitiable to boot. If justly—unenviable.

Polus. It is he rather who dies unjustly who is pitiable and miserable.

Socrates. Less than the slayer, O Polus, and less than he who justly dies.

Polus. What does this mean, Socrates?

Socrates. This—that the greatest of all evils is to commit a wrong.

Polus. Is this indeed the greatest? and is it not a greater to be wronged?

Socrates. No, by no means.

Polus. You forsooth would wish to be wronged rather than to wrong?

Socrates. I would wish for neither; but if it were inevitable either to wrong or to be wronged, I would choose rather to be wronged than to wrong.

Polus. You, then, would not take to yourself a tyranny?

Socrates. No, if by tyranny you mean the same as I do.

Polus. I mean, of course, the same as I meant before, namely to be able to do in the city whatever seems good to oneself, and to slay and banish, and do all things according to one's own bent.

.   .   .   .

469d.

(Socrates by illustration makes Polus admit that an ordinary individual thus doing what seems good to him would be treated as a malefactor—and from this reaches the conclusion, first, that only when doing as one likes brings some advantage is it regarded as a good, finally that the action which is good is that which is done justly, and when unjustly it is evil. Polus tries to evade this result by an appeal to common opinion. It is difficult to confute Socrates, yet even a child could show that he is not saying what is true. In spite of the great crimes of Archelaus all the Athenians would envy his power and prosperity. Socrates allows this, but rejects the appeal to numbers. This sort of argument is rhetorical and has nothing to do with truth. The matter must be considered in another way.)

472c.

Socrates. Indeed the subject in dispute is no small one,

it is little else than the question knowledge of which is beyond all price, and ignorance worst of all For the sum of
the matter is to know or not to know who it is that has and
who that lacks true happiness. For example, first to take
the case we are now discussing, you think that a man can
be happy when committing wrong and injustice, since you
suppose that Archelaus was both unjust and happy. Are we
not to understand that you are of this opinion?

Polus. Certainly.

Socrates. And I for my part say that this is impossible.
Here is one point on which we differ. Well then, will he
be happy in his wrong-doing if he meets with judgment
and punishment?

Polus. Certainly not, for in that case he would be most
miserable.

Socrates. But if the wrong-doer does not suffer punishment, according to your argument he will be happy?

Polus. That's what I say.

Socrates. According to my view, Polus, the wrong-doer
and the unjust, wretched as he is from every point of view,
will be more wretched still if he do not make atonement,
nor meet with retribution, but less wretched if he make
atonement and meet with judgment from gods and men.

Polus. What a paradoxical position you take, Socrates!

Socrates. And I shall try to make even you also, my
comrade, agree with me, for I look on you as a well-wisher.
At present these are the points on which we differ. Examine
them yourself. I said above that to commit wrong was a
greater evil than to be wronged.

.   .   .   .   .   .

Polus. How? If a man is taken in the act when aiming
at a tyranny and having been seized is tortured and wounded,
has his eyes burnt out, and suffers many other great outrages of all kinds, and having beheld his children and his wife

maltreated, last of all is crucified, or burnt in pitch, will such an one be more blest than if escaping scot-free he is established in power, and ruling in the city spends his life doing what he will, envied and accounted happy by citizens, and all others?

Socrates. You are scaring us with horrors, my excellent Polus, and not refuting. Now, remind me of your points. Suppose a man unjustly aims at a tyranny, you were saying?

Polus. I was.

Socrates. In no sense, then, will either be more happy than the other, neither he who justly secures the tyranny, nor he who meets with chastisement. For since both are miserable, there would not exist a happier of the two. More miserable, however, is he who escapes punishment, and gains the tyranny. What is this, Polus? Do you laugh? A strange sort of refutation is this when one makes a statement to laugh at it. It is not to refute.

Polus. Don't you find yourself confuted, Socrates, when you say things of this kind which no human being would grant? Ask then any of these present.

(Socrates again rejects the appeal to the many. He is not a politician and does not understand it. He is content if he can convince the person with whom he is rationally discussing.)

474b.

Socrates. I then believe that both I and you and other men think to commit wrong a greater evil than to suffer it, and not to be punished for the wrong a greater evil than to be punished.

Polus. Whilst I hold that neither I nor any other man thinks this; though you would rather suffer wrong than do it.

Socrates. You also, and all others——

Polus. Far from it, neither I nor anyone else.

Socrates. Will you not answer?

Polus. Certainly. For I want to know whatever you can mean——

474c.

Socrates. Reply to me then, so that you may know, just as if I were starting afresh to question you. Whether does it seem to you, Polus, a greater evil to commit injustice or to suffer it?

Polus. To suffer it, I say.

Socrates. What then? Which is more shameful, to commit or to suffer injustice?

Polus. To commit it.

Socrates. Would it not then be a greater evil, if more shameful?

Polus. Decidedly not.

Socrates. I see. It appears that you do not regard as equivalent the noble and the good, and the bad and the shameful.

Polus. Indeed no.

Socrates. What do you say to this? In respect to all beautiful things, such as bodies and colours, and forms and sounds, and ways of life, without looking any further, do we not call them severally beautiful in relation to something else? As for instance, first, beautiful bodies, is it not the case that you call them beautiful on account of the use with reference to which each is useful, or on account of some pleasure when the beholding of them gives pleasure to the beholders? Can you mention any other point than these in connection with physical beauty?

Polus. Not I.

474d, e.

(It is agreed that the same holds good of all things that are beautiful—forms, colours, sounds, music, laws and customs, sciences. They are all beautiful either through their utility, or the pleasure they give.)

.   .   .   .   .   .

475a.

Socrates. And do we not define the base in an opposite way, by the pain and evil it causes?

Polus. Necessarily so.

Socrates. Whenever, then, of two beautiful things one is the more beautiful, it is so in virtue of excelling either in one of these properties or in both, namely in its pleasure-giving or useful quality, or in both?

Polus. Unquestionably.

Socrates. And whenever one of two shameful things is the more shameful, it will be so through excelling either in its pain-giving or worthless qualities? Does not this follow?

Polus. Yes.

Socrates. Well then, what was it you said just now in regard to doing and suffering injustice? Did you not say that to suffer injustice was a greater evil, but to commit injustice a greater baseness?

Polus. I did.

475b.

Socrates. And if to commit injustice is more base than to suffer it, it is either more painful or more evil, and by exceeding in pain or in evil or in both is more base. Shall we then first enquire whether to be unjust exceeds in pain the suffering of injustice and whether those who are unjust feel more pain than those who suffer wrong?

Polus. Never, O Socrates, is it thus!

Socrates. Injustice does not then surpass in pain?

Polus. Of course not.

Socrates. If not then in pain, it would not exceed in both respects?

Polus. It appears not.

Socrates. Is not, therefore, the other property left?

Polus. Yes.

Socrates. That is evil?

Polus. So it seems.

475C.

Socrates. It is therefore through exceeding in evil that to commit injustice is worse than to suffer it?

Polus. Evidently it is.

Socrates. And was it not agreed both by the majority of people and by you, in our former discourse, that to do injustice is baser than to suffer it?

Polus. Yes.

Socrates. Now, therefore, it is shown to be a greater evil?

Polus. It seems so.

Socrates. Would you then accept rather the greater evil and baseness, instead of the less? Do not hesitate to answer, Polus; for it will do you no harm. But submitting to reason, even as to a physician, give your answer. Do you affirm or deny what I ask?

Polus. Well—I should not accept it, Socrates.

475e.

Socrates. And would any other man?

Polus. Not, as it appears to me, according to this argument.

Socrates. I speak the truth, therefore, when I say that neither I, nor you, nor any other man would choose rather to wrong than to be wronged; for it turns out to be a greater evil?

Polus. So it seems.

. . . .

476.

Socrates. Next in order let us examine the question about which in the second place we disagreed; whether it is the greatest evil for the wrong-doer to suffer the penalty, as you thought, or a greater not to suffer it, as I supposed.

(The first part of the argument which follows is based on the principle that in any act, the quality present in the act is present also in that which is acted upon. Hence, since he who punishes wrong-doing does justly, the wrong-doer likewise suffers justly, and therefore suffers something of beauty and value. This leads on to another stage of the argument.)

477a.

Socrates. The soul becomes better if it is justly punished?

Polus. Likely enough.

Socrates. For is not the soul which suffers the penalty delivered from baseness?

Polus. Yes.

Socrates. Nay, is it not released from the greatest evil? Look at it in this way. In connection with a man's condition, as regards money, do you contemplate any evil other than poverty?

Polus. No—only poverty.

Socrates. How about the culture of the body? The evil contemplated you would say to be weakness, and disease, and deformity, and the like?

Polus. I should.

477b.

Socrates. Do you not suppose that there is also a bad condition of the soul?

Polus. Why should there not be?

Socrates. And would you not call this injustice, and ignorance, and cowardice, and vices of this kind?

Polus. Assuredly.

Socrates. Have you not, therefore, said that in connection with these three things—money, the body, and the soul—" there are three evils, poverty, disease, injustice"?

Polus. Yes.

Socrates. Which then of the evils is the most hateful? Is it not injustice and, in short, the evil of the soul?

Polus. Certainly.

Socrates. And if the most hateful, the most evil.

Polus. What are you saying, Socrates?

477c.

Socrates. This, that according to the position reached earlier, that which is most shameful is always so because it produces the greatest pain or injury, or both.

Polus. Most certainly.

Socrates. And it was agreed by us just now that injustice and the evil of the soul in general is the most shameful?

Polus. It was agreed.

Socrates. Is it not then either the most painful and exceeding in pain, or exceeding in the mischief it does, or in both?

Polus. Necessarily so.

Socrates. But are injustice, licentiousness, cowardice, ignorance more painful than poverty and sickness?

Polus. It does not seem so to me, O Socrates, from our premises.

Socrates. It is then in a certain great injuriousness and amazing evil that the wickedness of the soul exceeds, surpassing other evils, most shameful of all, since according to your conception it is not in painfulness that it exceeds?

477e.

Polus. Apparently.

Socrates. But surely that which exceeds in the greatest harmfulness must be the greatest evil in the world?

Polus. Yes.

Socrates. Injustice then and vice, and every other kind of wickedness in the soul, is the greatest of all evils?

Polus. It appears so.

Socrates. What is the art which delivers from poverty? Is it not money-making?

Polus. Yes.

Socrates. And from disease?—Medicine?

Polus. Necessarily so.

Socrates. And from wickedness and injustice? If you are

not yet able to answer, look at it from this point of view—where and to whom do we take those who are sick in the body?

478a.

Polus. To the physicians, Socrates.

Socrates. And where do we take the wrong-doers and licentious?

Polus. To the judges, you mean?

Socrates. In order that they may submit to punishment.

Polus. I agree.

Socrates. Well, do not those who punish rightly exercise a form of justice?

Polus. Obviously.

Socrates. It is then money-making which releases from poverty, medicine from disease, the court of justice from vice and wrong-doing?

Polus. It seems so.

Socrates. Which of these is the noblest?

Polus. Of what things are you speaking?

Socrates. Money-making, medicine, the court of justice.

Polus. The court of justice by far, Socrates.

478b.

Socrates. If then it is the noblest, either it causes the greatest pleasure or benefit, or both?

Polus. Yes.

Socrates. But is the process of undergoing a medical cure pleasant, and do those who undergo it enjoy themselves?

Polus. I don't think so.

Socrates. But it is useful, is it not?

Polus. Yes.

Socrates. For they are delivered from a great evil, so that it profits them to endure the pain and regain health?

Polus. How could it be otherwise?

Socrates. Now would a man who has been cured be in

the happier bodily condition, or he who had not been ill at all?

Polus. Clearly he who had never been ill.

Socrates. It is not then happiness, apparently, to be released from evil, but never to have possessed it?

Polus. That is so.

Socrates. What of this? Which is the more miserable of two who have an evil, whether in the body or the soul, he who is cured and delivered from the evil, or he who is not cured and still has it?

Polus. He who is not cured, as it seems to me.

Socrates. Was it not agreed that the release from the greatest evil—wickedness—lies in suffering the punishment?

Polus. It was.

Socrates. For the punishment creates a better mind and makes the offenders more just, and corresponds to the cure of wickedness?

Polus. Yes.

478e.

Socrates. Happiest of all then is he who has no wickedness in his soul, since this is seen to be the greatest of evils?

Polus. Evidently.

Socrates. In the second place, I suppose, the man who is relieved of his wickedness?

Polus. So it appears.

Socrates. And this was the man who has been chastened and chastised, and has paid the penalty?

Polus. Yes.

Socrates. The worst life then is lived by the man who is of a bad character and not delivered from it?

Polus. Apparently.

Socrates. And is this not the man who, committing the greatest wrongs, and practising the greatest injustice, goes on his way without being rebuked or punished, or paying the penalty, as you say Archelaus contrived to do, and other tyrants, and orators, and rulers?

Polus. It would look like it.

Socrates. For almost the same thing, my good friend, has happened in the case of these men, as if someone afflicted with the greatest diseases should go on his way not rendering to the physicians the penalty for his bodily misdemeanours nor being cured, fearing like a child the burning and the cutting, because they are painful. Or don't you think so too?

Polus. I do.

Socrates. They are ignorant, apparently, what sort of a thing is the health and excellence of the body. According to the position we have now reached, those who flee from justice run the risk of doing this sort of thing, O Polus, that is, of observing what is painful in it, whilst they are blind to what is beneficial. They are ignorant, by how much more wretched it is than having an unhealthy body—to dwell with a soul that is not healthy, but rotten, and unjust, and unholy. Hence they do everything possible not to pay the penalty and be delivered from the greatest evil, getting together both money and friends, and preparing to speak with the most persuasive power. If our premises are true, Polus, do you perceive the conclusions of the argument, or would you prefer that we should sum them up?

Polus. Unless you would rather not.

Socrates. Well then, injustice and to commit wrong is the greatest evil?

Polus. It appears so.

Socrates. And deliverance from this evil is to suffer punishment?

Polus. Agreed.

Socrates. And failure to suffer the penalty means the persistence of the evil?

Polus. Yes.

Socrates. To be unjust is the second greatest evil, whilst to be unjust without paying the penalty for it is the greatest and chief of all evils?

Polus. So it seems.

Socrates. Now then, my friend, was not this point at issue between us: On the one hand you congratulated on his happiness Archelaus, a man who whilst committing the greatest wrongs did not suffer punishment for them; I, on the other hand, maintaining the opposite, that whether Archelaus or any other man does wrong without being punished, it is his portion to be miserable beyond other men, and that the wrong-doer is always more miserable than the wronged, and he who does not pay the penalty for it than he who does? Were these not my positions?

Polus. Yes.

Socrates. And has the truth of what was said been accepted?

Polus. I suppose so.

(Socrates applies the principle to the subject of Rhetoric, with which the dialogue began. Rhetoric is useless in defence of any wrong committed, but might well be used for the accusation and bringing to justice of wrong-doers. If we want to avenge ourselves on our enemy we must do our best to prevent his cure by punishment—even to the point of making him immortal, if he be deserving of death, or at least giving him as long a life as possible.)

Callicles. Do tell me, Chaerophon, if Socrates is in earnest, or joking?

Chaerophon. He seems to me, Callicles, to be in deadly earnest. But as the proverb says, there is nothing like asking him himself.

Callicles. But by Heaven, that's what I want to do. Tell me, O Socrates, whether we are to say that you are serious now or joking? For if you are serious, and what you are saying should happen to be true, would anything else result but that the life of us men has been upside down, and that, as it would seem, we are doing everything opposite to what we ought to do?

482.

(Socrates welcomes the entrance of Callicles into the discussion. Callicles begins by pointing out that Socrates has taken an unfair advantage of Polus, and made him appear inconsistent, because Polus is hampered by shame or respect for convention.)

The Opposition of Nature and Law or Convention

Callicles. I do not admire Polus for conceding to you that to do wrong is baser than to suffer wrong. As a result of this, entangled by you, he was tripped up in his argument, ashamed to say what he thought. You however, Socrates, really bring forward this kind of vulgar and popular illustration professing to pursue the truth, and speaking of what is noble when it is not noble according to nature, but by custom. Now these two are almost universally contrary to each other, nature and convention. And if one feels ashamed, and does not dare to say what he thinks, he is constrained to the saying of the opposite. And you having contrived this artifice, use trickery in your arguments; when someone speaks from the standpoint of what is customary, insinuating that of nature, if he mean nature, assuming that it is custom. As for instance in these notions, wronging and being wronged. Whilst Polus was speaking of what is base according to custom, you went on to argue from what he meant in a conventional sense, as if it meant according to nature.

Now by nature the more base is always the same as the more injurious, in this case to suffer the wrong, but conventionally to do the wrong is baser. Nor is it the part of a man to be wronged, but of a sort of slave, for whom it is better to die than to live, since when wronged and abused, he is neither able to defend himself, nor anyone else who is of concern to him. But I think that those who establish laws are the weak people and the majority. Therefore they frame the laws in relation to themselves and their own interest, and determine by their approval what is approved, and by their disapproval what is disapproved. And since they are in fear of those who are stronger and able to take the greater share, in order that these may not take a greater share they declare that it is base and unjust to take more, and that this is injustice to seek to have more than others. They are pleased themselves, I suppose, if they have an equal share, since they are more worthless. On this account it is the having a superiority over the masses, which is called unjust and base by social convention.

But as I think, nature herself demonstrates that justice lies in the better having more than the worse, and the more powerful than the less powerful. That this is so may be seen everywhere, both amongst animals and in all the cities of men and nations, and that what is just is decided in this way, that the better should rule the worse, and have the advantage. For what other right did Xerxes exercise when he marched against Greece, or his father against the Scythians, or the countless other examples of this kind which one might cite? But in my opinion these men act thus in accordance with what is just by nature, and by Heaven, in accordance with law, namely that of nature; not perhaps, however, in accordance with the law which we make, forcing into a mould the best and strongest of ourselves, taking them from youth up, soothing and enchanting them as trainers do lions, and enslaving them by teaching that we must have equality, and this is what is noble and just. But when, as I expect, there will arise a man having a nature sufficient for the task, shaking off all this, breaking through, and escaping, trampling under foot our writings and juggleries, and spells, and laws, all those which are against nature, rising up he will display himself as our lord, who was a slave, and there will shine forth the justice of nature. It seems to me that Pindar expressed what I am saying in the Ode in which he says that

> Custom is of all things Lord,
> Mortal and immortal.

And again he says:

> The most powerful justly leads with overmastering hand—I call the deeds of Hercules to witness.

For not because of purchase nor the gift of Geryon—something like this it runs (I do not know the Ode)—did Hercules drive away the cattle, natural justice being this, that oxen and all other possessions of the worse and weaker people should belong to the better and stronger.

That this is the truth, you will learn and turn to higher things, leaving philosophy. For philosophy, Socrates, is a charming pursuit, if one engages in it with moderation in youth; but if it is pursued farther than is suitable, it becomes the destruction of men.

(Socrates, delighted to have such a bold adversary, observes that the enquiry on which they are engaged is the most excellent of all —what a man ought to be and do, both in age and youth. He proceeds to try and make Callicles define what he means by stronger. Not, it seems, merely physical strength, since the many would have this more than the few, in virtue of their numbers. Callicles is thus led to say that the stronger are the better, wiser, more capable of rule. Are they to rule themselves, *i.e.*, be temperate and self-controlled? No, for the happy man must be slave to no one, not even himself. He must let his desires be as great as possible, and use his courage and wisdom to minister to them.)

492e.

Socrates. Those, then, do not speak truly who say that the happy are they who feel the lack of nothing.

Callicles. Stones, forsooth, would in that case be the happiest beings, and the dead.

Socrates. And certainly, as you mean, a fearful thing would life be. And yet I should not be surprised if Euripides spoke truly when he said: " Who knoweth, whether life may not be death, and death be life? "

I

And we ourselves in reality are now dead. Indeed, I also have heard from wise men that we now are dying, and the body is our tomb. That part of the soul in which the desires are, is something easily persuaded and swayed up and down. And someone speaking mythically, a discerning man (perhaps a Sicilian or Italian), because the words for *persuade* and *jar* are similar, varying the word called it a jar, and the unintelligent they called uninitiated. In the case of the uninitiated, this element of the soul to which the desires belong, they call the unbridled—likening it to a jar with holes, on account of its insatiate desires. Contrary to you, O Callicles, it is shown that of those who dwell in Hades (meaning the Unseen), these uninitiated are the most wretched, and that they carry to the pierced jar, water in another such pierced sieve. Now by the sieve, as he said who spoke of this to me, we are to understand the soul. He likened the soul of the uninitiated, as a thing that is pierced, to a sieve, since it is not able to enclose itself, on account of lack of belief and forgetfulness. This is very likely an odd simile. It makes clear, however, what I want to demonstrate to you, if I am in any way able to persuade you to change your view, and prefer to the unsatisfied and intemperate life, the orderly life, sufficient, holding itself ready in all circumstances.

(Socrates' illustrations do not convince Callicles, who avers that the life which is like a filled jar has no pleasure, but is the life of a stone. A pleasant life consists in the greatest possible flux, or the possession of all desires and capacity to satisfy them. A discussion follows on pleasure. Is it the same as the good? Socrates is able to prove that they are not the same, after Callicles has admitted a standard by allowing that some pleasures are better than others. The discussion ranges over the nature of the arts of flute-playing, tragedy, rhetoric, with a view to proving that the object of all these should be to make people better; and Socrates denies that even Themistocles, Cimon, Miltiades, or Pericles, used their powers to this end and not to flatter the people. Finally, the nature of the good is further defined.)

503d.

The good man, when speaking with a view to what is

best, will surely speak not at random, but with his mind fixed
on something? Similarly all other workers, each having his
attention fixed on his work, will not choose at random any
addition to it, but only with a view to giving some definite
form to that which he is fashioning. So if you will look at
the painters, architects, ship-builders, and all other craftsmen—any of them you like—you will see how each lays in a
definite place whatever he brings, and forces the one to be
suitable to the other and harmonise with it, until the whole
construction is fashioned and symmetrically put together.
And so with other workers, and those of whom we spoke
just now, who have to do with the body, gymnastic teachers
and physicians. They bring the body into order and system.

.   .   .   .   .   .

504b.

What of the soul? Will it be serviceable if disorderly, or
when there is order and system?

Callicles. This must be admitted on our premises.

Socrates. It seems to me that we call healthy the orderly
state of the body, from which health develops in it, and other
bodily virtues. For the orderly condition and harmony of
the soul, the names are law-abiding and law, whence come
what is law-abiding and orderly. Now these are justice and
temperance.

Will not, then, that orator who is expert and good, ever
look to this in all that he does, when bringing his teaching
to bear on the soul, and in all his doing, and the gifts that
he gives, and in what he takes away, ever bending his mind to
this end, how he shall produce justice and temperance in the
minds of the citizens, and deliver them from injustice, and
intemperance, and how all other virtue may develop, and
vice flee away?

The Ideal as Eternal Beauty

Symposium. From Socrates' report of the speech of the Prophetess Diotima. Greek Text: R. G. Bury's Edition. The following translation is by Shelley (1792–1822).

Diotima. Your own meditations, O Socrates, might have initiated you in all these things which I have already taught you on the subject of love. But those perfect and sublime ends to which these are only means, I know not that you would have been competent to discover. I will declare them, therefore, and will render them as intelligible as possible. Do you, meanwhile, strain all your attention to trace the obscure depth of the subject.

He who aspires to love rightly, ought from his earliest youth to seek an intercourse with beautiful forms, and first, if his leader rightly leads, to make a single form the object of his love, and therein to generate intellectual excellences. He ought, then, to consider that beauty, in whatever form it resides, is the brother of that beauty which subsists in another form, and if he ought to pursue that which is beautiful in form, it would be absurd to imagine that beauty is not one and the same thing in all forms, and would therefore remit much of his ardent preference towards one, through his perception of the multitude of claims upon his love. In addition, he would consider the beauty which is in souls more excellent than that which is in the body, so that one endowed with an admirable soul, even though the flower of the form were withered, would suffice him as the object of his love and care, and the companion with whom he might seek and produce such conclusions as tend to the improvement of youth; so that he might be led to observe the beauty and the conformity which there is in morals and the laws, and to

perceive that all this is akin to him, and to esteem little the
mere beauty of the outward form.

He would then conduct his pupil to science, so that
he might look upon the loveliness of wisdom; and that
contemplating thus the universal beauty, no longer would
he unworthily and meanly enslave himself to the attrac-
tions of one object in love, nor one subject of discipline
or science, but would turn towards the wide ocean of
intellectual beauty, and from the sight of the many
lovely and majestic thoughts which it contains, would
abundantly bring forth his conceptions in philosophy; until
strengthened and confirmed, he should at length steadily
contemplate one science, which is the science of this universal
beauty. Attempt, I entreat you, to mark what I say with as
keen an observation as you can. He who has been disciplined
to this point in love by contemplating beautiful objects
gradually and in their order, now arriving at the end of all
that concerns love, on a sudden beholds a beauty wonderful
in its nature. This is it, O Socrates, for the sake of which all
the former labours were endured. It is eternal, unproduced,
indestructible, neither subject to increase, nor decay: not
like other things partly beautiful and partly deformed; not
at one time beautiful and at another time not; not beautiful
in relation to one thing and deformed in relation to another;
not here beautiful and there deformed. Nor can this supreme
beauty be figured to the imagination like a beautiful face or
beautiful hands or any portion of the body, nor like any
discourse, nor any science, nor does it subsist in anything
else such as an animal, nor is either in earth, nor in heaven,
nor in any other place; but it is eternally uniform and consistent and unique. All other things are beautiful through a
participation in it, with this condition that although they are
subject to production and decay, it never becomes more or
less or endures any change.

When anyone ascending from a pure type of love begins to contemplate this supreme beauty, he already approaches consummation of his labour. For such as discipline themselves upon this system, or are conducted by another, beginning to ascend through those transitory objects which are beautiful towards that which is beauty itself, proceed as on steps from the love of one form to that of two, and from that of two to that of all objects which are beautiful, and from beautiful forms to beautiful morals, and from morals to beautiful doctrines; until from the meditation of many doctrines, they arrive at that which is nothing else than the doctrine of the supreme beauty itself in the knowledge and contemplation of which at length they repose. " Such a life as this, my dear Socrates," exclaimed the stranger prophetess, " spent in the contemplation of the beautiful, is the life for men to live; which if you chance ever to experience, you will esteem far beyond gold and rich garments, and even those lovely persons whom you and many others now gaze on with astonishment, and are prepared neither to eat nor drink so that you may behold and live for ever with these objects of your love! What, then, shall we imagine to be the aspect of the supreme beauty itself, simple, pure, uncontaminated with the inter-mixture of human flesh and colours, and all other idle and unreal shapes attendant on mortality, the divine, the original, the supreme, the unique beauty? What must be the life of him who dwells with and gazes on that which it becomes us all to seek? Think you not that to him alone is accorded the prerogative of bringing forth not images and shadows of virtue, for he is in contact not with a shadow, but with reality, with virtue itself, in the production and nourishment of which he becomes dear to the gods, and if such a privilege is conceded to any human being, himself immortal?"

P. B. SHELLEY.

Republic

Plato's *Republic* begins with a discussion of the nature of justice, and develops into a consideration of the Ideal State, since, according to Socrates, perfect justice can only be seen at work in the perfectly organised community. Later it is disclosed that the philosophic statesmen who are to preside over the community in its political and moral life, must have, to equip them for the task, a vision and understanding of the principle of the "Good," source of all things in the universe. The nature of the philosopher and his training are therefore investigated, and the theory of the Ideas or eternal forms of all goodness, beauty, justice (as well as of other general conceptions) explained by Socrates. The passages which follow are chosen as the most illuminating in regard to the ethical substance of this dialogue, often thought to be Plato's greatest work, and certainly the best known.

Sophistic Theories of Justice

THE REPUBLIC ii. 353. Greek Text: Jowett and Campbell's Edition. Translation by A. D. Lindsay (Master of Balliol).

(Socrates' young friends, Glaucon and Adeimantus, wish to make him realise that he is expected to prove that Justice is the greatest good for him who is just, even though he gain nothing else by it, but rather loses everything that is usually prized. They put before him, therefore, the views openly expressed by popular thinkers and tacitly accepted by the majority, if we are to judge by their acts when they have the opportunity, and by the form of their praise and blame, whether of righteous or unrighteous conduct. For the standard of praise seems determined by the success rather than the goodness of a life, and if virtue unsuccessful is nevertheless approved, it is with a view to rewards hereafter.)

Glaucon. " Listen, then, and I shall begin as I proposed with the nature and origin of justice. By nature, men say, to do injustice is good, to suffer it, evil; but there is more evil in suffering injustice than there is good in inflicting it. Therefore when men act unjustly towards one another, and thus experience both the doing and the suffering, those amongst them who are unable to compass the one and escape the other, come to this opinion: that it is more profitable that they should mutually agree neither to inflict injustice nor to suffer it. Hence men began to establish laws and covenants with one another, and they called what the law prescribed lawful and just. This, then, is the origin and nature of justice. It is a mean between the best—doing injustice with impunity—and the worst—suffering injustice without possibility of requital. Thus justice, being a mean between those extremes, is looked upon with favour, not because it is good, but because the inability to inflict injustice makes it valuable. For no one who had the power to inflict injustice and was anything of a man would ever make a contract of mutual abstention from injustice with anyone else. He would be mad if he did. Such, Socrates, is the nature of justice, and such is its origin, according to the popular account."

(As an example of the Unjust Man, Glaucon describes the career of Gyges the Lydian, who became possessed of a ring which rendered him invisible, and having through this a power beyond that of other men immediately used it to obtain by wrong and violence a kingdom and all that he desired. Thus "everyone is unjust whenever he thinks injustice possible.")

Picture of the Just Man

361.

"Beside him, in accordance with the argument, let us place our just man, a simple and noble character, one who, as Aeschylus says, desires not to seem, but to be good. The semblance, indeed, we must take from him; for if he is reputed just, he will enjoy the honours and rewards that such a reputation earns, and thus it will not be apparent, it is objected, whether he is just for justice' sake or the honours' and rewards' sake. He must be stripped of everything except justice, and made the very counterpart of the other man. He shall do no injustice and be reputed altogether unjust, that his justice may be tested as being proof against ill-repute and its consequences, and he go on his way unchanged till death, all his life seeming unjust but being just. Thus these two will have come to the extremes of justice and of injustice, and we may judge which of them is the happier."

"Halloo, my dear Glaucon," I said, "how energetically you are scouring these two for judgment, as if they were a pair of statues."

"I am doing my best," he said. "Well, given two such characters, it is not difficult now, I fancy, to go on to discover what sort of life awaits each of them. Let me describe it. If my description is rather harsh, remember, Socrates, that those who praise injustice above justice are responsible, and not I. They will say that our just man will be scourged, racked, fettered, will have his eyes burnt out, and at last, after all manner of suffering, will be crucified and will learn that he ought to desire not to be but to seem just; for those words of Aeschylus applied much more truly to the unjust man. For it is the unjust man in reality they will say, who, as his practice is akin to truth, and his life not ruled by appearances, desires not to seem but to be unjust.

> And from the deep ploughed furrow of his heart
> Reaps harvest rich of goodly purposes."

(Adeimantus takes up the argument and illustrates from poets and other authorities the contention that it is not the reality but the cloak of justice which is respected. He concludes with an appeal to Socrates.)

367.

Adeimantus. "I can put up with others praising justice and condemning injustice in this way, eulogising and reviling the respective reputations and rewards they bring, but not with your doing so, unless you insist on it, for you have spent all your life on this one enquiry. Therefore do not be content with proving to us that justice is stronger than injustice, but show what effect they each have on their possessors, that makes them in themselves and by themselves, whether or not they be hid from gods and men, the one good and the other bad."

The Lie in the Soul

(This conception belongs to the Platonic form of the doctrine that virtue is knowledge. He who is incapable of seeing the truth in regard to what is real in the world, who has a wrong view of what matters in life, has the most fatal blindness or darkness in his soul.)

THE REPUBLIC ii. 382.

Socrates. " Do you not know," I said, " that all gods and men hate the true lie, if we may use the expression? "

" What do you mean? " he said.

" This," I said. " No one deliberately wishes to lie in the most vital part of him about the most vital matters. Everyone fears above all to harbour a lie in that quarter."

" I don't yet understand," he said.

" That is because you think I am uttering some mysterious truth. All I am saying is that to lie, and be the victim of a lie, and to be ignorant in the soul concerning reality, to hold and possess falsehood there, is the last thing any man would desire. Men hate falsehood in such a case above all."

" Certainly," he said.

" But this that I have just mentioned may be most accurately called the true lie, namely, the ignorance in the soul of him who is deluded; since the spoken lie is an imitation of this state in the soul, an image of it which arises afterwards and is not a wholly unmixed lie. Is it not so? "

" Certainly."

" Then the real lie is hated not only by the gods, but also by men? "

" I think so."

The Young must be nurtured in a Beautiful Environment

(The capacity of discerning what is good in life and the love for it, will only come to those whose emotions have been rightly guided in youth by meeting the experiences that harmonise with their best aspirations, and not with the lower impulses.)

THE REPUBLIC iii. 401.

" For we would not have our guardians reared among

images of evil as in a foul pasture, and there day by day and little by little gather many impressions from all that surrounds them, taking them all in until at last a great mass of evil gathers in their inmost souls, and they know it not. No, we must seek out those craftsmen who have the happy gift of tracing out the nature of the fair and graceful, that our young men may dwell as in a health-giving region, where all that surrounds them is beneficent, whencesoever from fair works of art there smite upon their eyes and ears an affluence like a wind bringing health from happy regions, which though they know it not, leads them from their earliest years into likeness and friendship and harmony with the principle of beauty."

" A nobler manner of education," he said, " there could not be."

" Then, Glaucon," I said, " is not musical education of paramount importance for those reasons, because rhythm and harmony enter most powerfully into the innermost part of the soul and lay forcible hands upon it, bearing grace with them, so making graceful him who is rightly trained, and him who is not, the reverse? Is it not a further reason that he who has been rightly trained in that city would be quick to observe all works of art that were defective or ugly, and all natural objects that failed in beauty? They would displease him, and rightly: but beautiful things he would praise, and receiving them with joy into his soul, would be nourished by them and become noble and good. Ugly things he would rightly condemn, and hate even in his youth before he was capable of reason; but when reason comes he would welcome her as one he knows, with whom his training has made him familiar."

*The Object of the State—the Good of the Whole, not of any
one Part*

THE REPUBLIC iv. 419. This may be thought to express
Plato's political point of view, but it is also a very important moral
principle for him. In the ordinary sense of the term, there is nothing
individualistic in his ethical outlook. The ideal of self-development
often held to be characteristic of the Greeks is not Platonic, but
Aristotelian. The notion of wholeness, the value of the individual
life seen only in its relation to the whole of which it is a part, first
the State, then the Universe, appears in a great deal of Plato's
philosophy.

Here Adeimantus interposed with the remark: " How,
Socrates, will you answer a possible objection that you are
not making these men so very happy, and that this unhappiness is their own fault? Really, the city belongs to them, and
yet they enjoy none of the advantages of other rulers. These
own lands, build fine and magnificent houses, which they
furnish with an equal magnificence; they make their own
sacrifices to the gods and indulge in hospitality, and, briefly,
to come to what you mentioned, are in possession of silver
and gold and everything that is thought essential to a state
of blessedness. But your rulers, the objector will say, seem
established in the city just like paid auxiliaries, nothing but
a garrison."

.   .   .   .   .   .

420.
" I fancy," I said, " that we shall find what to say, if we
proceed along the path we have followed up till now. For
we shall say that while it would not surprise us if even
under these conditions these men were extremely happy,
still our purpose in founding the city was not to make any
one class in it surpassingly happy, but to make the city as
a whole as happy as possible. For it was our idea that in such a
city we should most certainly find justice, as we should find
injustice in the worst-governed city, and by inspecting both,
we hoped to decide our old question. And now we are, we

think, constructing the happy city, not in a partial way by making happy a few people in it, but by making happy the whole city."

Courage

THE REPUBLIC iv. 429. Plato's treatment of Courage illustrates the Socratic doctrine that the virtues are forms of wisdom or knowledge, but at the same time emphasises the necessity of emotional training.

Socrates. " I mean," I said, " that courage is a kind of safe-keeping."

" Yes, but what kind."

" The safe-keeping of the belief produced by law, through education, concerning the number and nature of things to be feared. By 'preserving throughout,' I meant preserving it and never losing it in pains and in pleasures, in desires and in fears. I will, if you like, illustrate it by a figure, which seems to me apt."

" Please do."

" You know, then," I said, " that when dyers want to dye wool purple, they first select from wools of different colours one particular kind, namely white; they then prepare the wool, treating it most elaborately in order that it may take the colour as well as possible, and then finally they put it in the dye. Wool that is dyed in this manner takes the dye in a most lasting way: no washing, whether with or without solvents, can take out the colour. But you know what happens when these precautions are neglected, when colours other than white are selected for dyeing, or when the white wool is not treated beforehand."

" I do," he said; " the colour washes out in a ridiculous way."

" Then," I said, " you may conceive that we, too, were following some such method to the best of our power when we selected the soldiers and educated them in music and gymnastic. Our purpose was simply that they should be dyed with the laws as beautifully as possible, so that with their possession of the proper nature and education, their belief both concerning things to be feared and other matters should be lasting. Their colour would then be impervious to those terribly effective solvents—pleasure, which works more powerfully than any potash or lye; and pain, and fear, and desire, which are stronger than any solvent in the world. Such a power of preserving throughout the right and lawful belief concerning what is and what is not to be feared, I define as courage, and give it that name if you do not object."

Temperance

THE REPUBLIC iv. 430.

"Temperance," I said, "is surely an ordering and a control of certain pleasures and desires, as is declared by the common but mysterious expression that a man is master of himself; and there are other similar expressions which give a clue to its nature. Do you not agree?"

"Most certainly," he said.

"But is not master of himself a ridiculous phrase? For he that is master of himself will surely also be slave of himself, and he that is slave, master; for the same person is mentioned in all these phrases."

"Undoubtedly."

"This expression, however," I said, "seems to me to mean that there is in the man himself, that is, in his soul, a better and a worse, and when the better has by nature control of the worse, then, as we say, the man is master of himself; for the expression is one of approval. When, on the other hand, in consequence of bad training, or the influence of associates, the better is weaker than the worse

and is overcome by its superior numbers, this is condemned
as something disgraceful, and the man who is in this condition
is called slave to himself, and intemperate."

"Yes, that is a probable explanation," he said.

. . . . . .

432.

"Temperance in its action is not like courage and wisdom.
The wisdom and the courage which make the city wise and
courageous reside each in a particular part, but temperance
is spread through the whole alike, setting in unison of the
octave the weakest and the strongest and the middle class
—a unison of wisdom, if you would have that; and strength,
if you would have that; of numbers also and wealth, and
any other such element. So that we may most justly say that
this unanimity is temperance, the concord of the naturally
worse and the naturally better as to which should rule in
the city or in the individual."

Justice

THE REPUBLIC iv. 433. Plato goes behind the ordinary conceptions of justice, such as that it lies in equality or in rendering to
all their deserts, and finds its essence in a principle which, if existing in the state, as in the soul of every citizen, would necessarily
create all conditions of justice in the people thus endowed, for the
performance of the true function by every member is the secret
of the harmony of the world.

In the State

Socrates. "At the beginning when we were founding our
city, the principle which we then stated should rule throughout, or at least a form of it, was I think justice. We stated
surely, and, if you remember, have often repeated our statement, that each individual should pursue that work in this
city for which his nature was naturally most fitted, each
man doing one work."

"Yes, we did."

" But we have often said ourselves, and heard others saying, that to mind one's own business and not be meddlesome is justice."

" Yes, we have."

" Well, then, my friend," I said, " this in some form or other is what justice seems to be, minding one's own business. Do you know how I infer this? "

" Do tell me," he said.

" We have examined," I said, " temperance and courage and wisdom, and I think that the remaining virtue in the city is that which enabled all these to find a place in it, and after they have appeared, preserves them so long as it is present in the city. But we said that if we found the first three, the remaining one would be justice."

" Yes, inevitably," he said.

" But," I said, " if we had to decide which of those virtues by its presence does most to make the city good, it would be hard to say whether it is the unanimity of rulers and ruled, or the preservation of lawful belief concerning what is and what is not to be feared, that makes its appearance among the soldiers, or the wisdom and guardianship of the rulers, which most contributes to the city's goodness; or whether, finally, it is not this principle abiding in child and woman, in slave and freeman and artisan, in ruler and ruled, that each minded his own business, one man one work, and was not meddlesome."

" It is, in truth, a hard question," he said.

" Then apparently the principle of each man doing his own business in a city competes in promoting that city's virtue with its wisdom and temperance and courage? "

" Certainly," he said.

" But would you not affirm that the principle which competes with these in promoting a city's virtue is justice? "

" Most assuredly."

Justice in the Individual Soul

THE REPUBLIC iv. 443.

Socrates. " The just man does not allow the different principles within him to do other work than their own, nor the distinct classes in his soul to interfere with one another: but in the truest sense he sets his house in order, gaining the mastery over himself, and becoming on good terms with himself through discipline, he joins in harmony those different elements, like three terms in a musical scale—lowest and highest and intermediate, and any others that may lie between those —and binding together all these elements, he moulds the many within him into one, temperate and harmonious. In this spirit he lives; whether he is money-making or attending to the wants of his body, whether he is engaged in politics or on business transactions of his own, throughout he considers and calls just and beautiful all conduct which pursues and helps to create this state of mind. The knowledge which superintends these actions is for him wisdom, while any conduct which tends to destroy this attitude is, for him, unjust, and the belief which inspires it, ignorance."

.   .   .   .   .   .

Virtue as Health

THE REPUBLIC iv. 444.

Socrates. " Now to produce health is to put the various parts of the body in their natural relations of authority or subservience to one another, while to produce disease is to disturb this natural relation."

" Yes."

" Then to produce justice," I said, " is to put the parts of the soul in their natural relations of authority or subservience, while to produce injustice is to disturb this natural relation, is it not? "

" Surely," he said.

K

" Then virtue, seemingly, will be a kind of health and beauty and good condition of the soul, vice a disease, and ugliness and weakness."

" That is true."

" Then do not fair practices conduce to the acquisition of virtue; ugly practices to the acquisition of vice? "

" Necessarily."

" There now apparently remains for us to inquire whether it is profitable to act justly and follow fair practices and be just, and that whether the just man is recognised as such or not, or whether acting unjustly and being unjust is profitable, even if the unjust man is not punished or reformed by correction."

" But, Socrates," he said, " this enquiry seems to me ridiculous at this stage, now that we have reached those respective conclusions about justice and injustice. People think that when the constitution of the body is ruined, life is not worth living, not with all the foods and drinks and wealth and dominion in the world; and are we to believe that, when the constitution of the very principle of our life is in confusion and ruin, life is then worth living, though a man do whatever he pleases—unless only he find some means of escaping from vice and injustice, and of acquiring justice and virtue? "

" Yes, it is ridiculous," I said.

The Dreaming and the Waking Life

THE REPUBLIC v. 476. In the more philosophic part of the *Republic*, when preparing the minds of his hearers for the conception of the eternal principle of "the good," without the vision of which human life cannot be well-ordered, either in the organisation of the state or the relations of individuals to each other, Socrates leads up to this by reference first to the idea of universal beauty which, as he elsewhere argues (*Phaedrus*), has the greatest vividness of all the ideas in its reflections in our experience.

Socrates. " On one side let us put lovers of sights and

lovers of crafts and men of action, and then on the other those with whom the argument is concerned, who alone are rightly called philosophers."

" What do you mean? " he said.

" Well," I said, " the lovers of sounds and of sights admire beautiful sounds and colours and figures and all things fashioned out of such, but their understanding is incapable of seeing or admiring the nature of real beauty."

" That is certainly the case," he said.

" Then will not those who are capable of approaching the real beauty and of seeing it as itself, be few in number? "

" Yes, indeed."

" But if a man recognises that there are beautiful things, but disbelieves in real beauty, and cannot follow, should another lead him to the knowledge of it, do you think that such an one leads a waking or a dreaming life? For, consider, is not a man dreaming, whether he is asleep or awake, when he thinks a likeness of anything to be not a likeness, but the reality which it resembles? "

" I certainly," he said, " should say that such a man was dreaming."

" But what of him who, contrariwise, recognises a certain real beauty, and is able to discern both it and the objects which participate in it, and does not take the participating objects for it or it for them, do you think he leads a waking or a dreaming life? "

" A waking life, most certainly," he said.

. . . . . .

479.

" Then we shall say that those who look at many beautifuls but do not see real beauty, and are unable to follow another's guidance to it, and who see many justs but not real justice, and so on, these throughout believe but know nothing of what they believe? "

" The conclusion is inevitable," he said.

" But what are we to say of those who look at all the invariable unchanging realities? Do they not know rather than believe? "

" That conclusion, too, is inevitable."

The Best if corrupted becomes the Worst

(Corruptio Optimi Pessima)

THE REPUBLIC vi. 491. The most gifted nature, with capacities for becoming both a moral and an intellectual genius, and of being the saviour of his people, the nature he calls philosophic, will, in Plato's view, if neglected in youth or corrupted by flattery and false teaching on life, become a greater source of evil than the petty nature with small endowments. The most dangerous corrupter of gifted youth, however, is not the individual tempter and false teacher or Sophist, but the crowd with its all-powerful plaudits and derision.

Socrates. " All things which are called good destroy and pervert the soul—beauty, riches, strength of body, powerful connections in a city, and all similar things. You understand the general type of the things I mean? "

" I do," he said, " but I should like to grasp your meaning more precisely."

" Well," I said, " grasp the notion of them as a whole, and what has been said about them will become perfectly clear and not seem paradoxical."

" What do you mean me to do? " he said.

" In the case of all seeds or growing things, whether plants or animals, we know," I said, " that any one which does not receive its proper nutriment, climate or habitat, fails in its proper virtues the more strikingly the stronger it is; for evil is of course more contrary to good than to what is not good."

" Surely."

" Then I fancy it is according to reason that the best

of natures deteriorates more seriously from uncongenial nutriment than an inferior nature?"

" It is."

" Then, Adeimantus," I said, " shall we not also say that similarly the most richly endowed natures, if they receive a bad upbringing, become surpassingly evil? Or do you fancy that great crimes and unmixed wickedness come from a feeble nature and not rather from a noble nature ruined by education, while a weak nature will never be the author of great good or great evil?"

" Yes, it is as you say," he said.

" Then I think that this nature which we have ascribed to the philosopher, if it receive proper instruction, must of necessity develop and attain to all virtue; but if it be not sown and planted in proper soil and get its nutriment therefrom, its course will be the very opposite, unless one of the gods come to the rescue. Or do you hold the opinion of the public that there are any appreciable number of young men corrupted by sophists; or that it is individual sophists who corrupt them? Are not those who say this themselves the greatest sophists, who most carefully educate and fashion to the character they want both young and old, men and women?"

" When, pray?" he said.

" When," I answered, " they sit down together in large numbers in the assemblies or the law courts, or the theatres or camps, or any other place where crowds come together, and proceed with great noise and confusion to find fault with some of the things that are being said or done, and to praise others, their fault-finding and their praise being equally extravagant, shouting and clapping their hands till the rocks and the place in which they are, join with them and echo back the redoubled uproar of their condemnation and their praise. Amid such a scene, where, think you, is a young man's heart? What private education will hold out and not be swamped by such a volume of condemnation and praise, and swept down stream wherever such a current take it, till he call beautiful and ugly what they do, act as they do, and become like them?"

In the Imperfect State the True Philosopher and Statesman is obliged to stand alone

THE REPUBLIC vi. 496. In these passages in which Plato (through the mouth of Socrates) is most uncompromising in his picture of the irreconcilability between the philosophic reformer and the actual state, he doubtless has always in his mind the treatment of Socrates by the Athenians. But if Xenophon's portrait of Socrates is true, at least as regards Socrates' own manner of life, he did not stand aside like Plato's philosopher in the actual (not ideal) city, but spent much of his time talking to his fellow-citizens of all types and social grades. He did, however, avoid politics as far as possible.

"Then, Adeimantus," I said, "a very small band is left of those who worthily associate with philosophy; possibly a noble and well-nurtured character saved by exile, which in the absence of corrupting influences has been true to its own nature and stayed by philosophy, or a great soul born in a small city, and so despising and looking beyond politics; and possibly one or two noble natures, might come to philosophy from some other art which they rightly despised. Then, again, the bridle of our comrade, Theages, might have constraining power. For Theages has all the endowments that might have induced him to desert philosophy except bodily health, and his feebleness of body keeps him from a political life. Of my own safeguard, the heavenly sign, we need not speak. For few, if any, before my time have had that. Now those who have become members of this small band, and have tasted the sweetness and blessedness of their prize, can all discern the madness of the many and the almost universal rottenness of all political actions. The philosopher sees that he has no ally with whose aid he might go and defend the right with a chance of safety. He is like a man in a den of wild beasts. Share their injustice he will not. He is not strong enough to hold out alone where all are savages. He would lose his life before he could do any benefit to the city or his friends, and so be equally useless to himself and to the world. Weighing all these considerations, he holds his peace and does his own work, like a man in a storm sheltering behind a wall from the driving wind of dust and hail. He sees other men filled with lawlessness, and is content if by any means he may live his life here unspotted by injustice and evil deeds, till with fair hope he takes his departure in peace and good-will."

"Well," he said, "he will certainly have accomplished not the least of things when he takes his departure."

"Yes," I said, "but not the greatest unless he finds a constitution suited to him."

The Idea or Form of the Good

THE REPUBLIC vi. 504. The question exactly how we are to understand Plato's conception of "the good" will probably always receive different answers. There will continue to be some who treat it as a principle for the unification of knowledge, and some who find in it Plato's Idea of God, and between these other varieties of interpretation. At least we may surely think of it as one way in which Plato expresses his conviction that human experience is unintelligible without the assumption that it is pervaded by a spiritual reality from which proceeds all that gives it meaning and value.

Socrates. " You have often heard that the Form of the good is the greatest study, and is that by whose use just things and the rest become helpful and useful. Now you certainly know that I was going to say this, and also that we have no proper knowledge of the Form of the good. And if we don't know it, though we should have the fullest knowledge possible of all else, you know that that would be of no use to us, any more than is the possession of anything without the good. Or do you think there is any advantage in universal possession if it is not good, or in understanding the whole world except the good, and understanding nothing that is good and beautiful?"

.   .   .   .   .   .

505.

"This, then, is that which every soul pursues, the motive of all its actions. That it is something the soul divines, but what it is, she can never in her perplexity fully comprehend. She has no steady confidence concerning it, as she has about other things, and therefore she loses any advantage she might have got from these. Concerning a subject so great and so important, can we say that the best men in our city, those to whom we shall entrust everything, ought to be unenlightened?"

"Certainly not," he said.

"I think, in any case," I said, "that if a man does not know how particular instances of justice and beauty are also good, these just and beautiful things will find in him a worthless guardian. For I divine that no man will know them thoroughly until he has acquired this knowledge."

"You divine excellently," he said.

"Then will our constitution be set in proper order if such a guardian, one who had this knowledge, direct it?"

"Inevitably," he said. "But for yourself, Socrates, do you say that the good is knowledge, or pleasure, or something else?"

(Socrates does not answer this question directly, but explains that the nature of the good can only be suggested by a simile. As the sun is in the visible world, source of light making possible both vision and the power of being seen, so is the idea of Good in the world of knowledge, in relation to mind and the objects known.)

508.

"You know," I said, "that when a man turns his eyes not to those objects on whose colours the light of day is shining, but to those where the lights of night shine, his eyes grow dim and appear almost blind, as though pure sight were not in them?"

"Yes, certainly," he said.

"But when they look at objects on which the sun is shining, I fancy that these same eyes see distinctly, and it becomes manifest that sight is in them?"

"Surely."

"Now consider the soul in this same manner. When it is stayed upon that on which truth and being are shining, it understands and knows and is seen to have reason. But when it is stayed on that which is mingled with darkness, that which is coming into being and passing away, then it believes and grows confused as its beliefs waver up and down, and has the appearance of being without reason."

"Yes, it has."

"This, then, which imparts truth to the things that are known and the power of knowing to the knower, you may affirm to be the Form of the good. It is the cause of knowledge and truth, and you may conceive it as being known, but while knowledge and truth are both beautiful, you will be right in thinking it other and fairer than these. And as in the other world it is right to think light and sight sunlike, but not right to think them the sun, so here it is right to think both knowledge and truth like the good, but not right to think either of them the good. The state or nature of the good must be honoured still more highly."

"You speak of an incalculable beauty," he said, "if it gives knowledge and truth, and itself excels them in beauty. Surely you do not mean that this is pleasure?"

"Do not blaspheme," I said.

The Cave-Dwellers

THE REPUBLIC vii. 514. In the myth of the Cave-dwellers Plato gives in a parable the essential thought of his interpretation of life, as also of knowledge and therefore of education. It may seem to be the interpretation of the mystics of all times, and yet many are the mystics and few are the Platonists. Very few, if any, among those for whom the things of experience are shadows or reflections of the unseen, and knowledge and goodness alike depend upon the cultivation of the vision of the reality behind phenomena, have based on this a logical scientific theory of knowledge and a practical discipline of education and life in Plato's manner.

Plato conveys in this allegory more vividly than elsewhere the truth his whole work expresses, that we have only to turn our eyes to the light and there will follow the transformation of the world for knowledge, and the transvaluation of all values, through which the salvation of man and society will come.

Socrates. "Then after this," I said, "liken our nature in its education and want of education to a condition which I may thus describe. Picture men in an underground cave-dwelling with a long entrance reaching up towards the light along the whole width of the cave; in this they lie from their childhood, their legs and necks in chains so that they stay where they are and look only in front of them, as the chain prevents them turning their heads round. Some way off and higher up, a fire is burning behind them, and between the fire and the prisoners is a road on higher ground. Imagine a wall built along this road like the screens which showmen have in front of the audience, over which they show the puppets."

"I have it," he said.

"Then picture also men carrying along this wall all kinds of articles, which overtop it—statues of men and other creatures in stone and wood and other materials; naturally some of the carriers are speaking; others are silent."

"A strange image and strange prisoners," he said.

"They are like ourselves," I answered. "For in the first place, do you think that such men would have seen anything of themselves or of each other except the shadows thrown by the fire on the wall of the cave opposite to them?"

"How could they," he said, "if all their life they had been forced to keep their heads motionless?"

"What would they have seen of the things carried along the wall? Would it not be the same?"

"Surely."

515.

"Then if they were able to talk to one another, do you not think that they would suppose what they saw to be the real things?"

"Necessarily."

"Then what if there were in their prison an echo from the opposite wall? When anyone of those passing by spoke, do you imagine that they could help thinking that the voice came from the shadow passing before them?"

"No, certainly not," he said.

"Then, most assuredly," I said, "the only truth that such men would conceive would be the shadows of those manufactured articles?"

"That is quite inevitable," he said.

"Then consider," I said, "the manner of their release from their bonds and the cure of their folly, supposing that they attained their natural destiny in some such way as this. Let us suppose one of them released, and forced suddenly to stand up and turn his head, and walk and look towards the light. Let us suppose, also, that all these actions gave him pain, and that he was too dazzled to see the objects whose shadows he had been watching before. What do you think he would say if he were told by someone that before he had been seeing mere foolish phantoms, while now he was nearer to being, and was turned to what in a higher degree is, and was looking more directly at it? And, further, if each of the several figures passing by were pointed out to him, and he were asked to say what each was, do you not think that he would be perplexed, and would imagine that the things he had seen before were truer than those now pointed out to him?"

" Yes, much truer," he said.

" Then, if he were forced to look at the light itself, would not his eyes ache, and would he not try to escape and turn back to things which he could look at, and think that they were really more distinct than the things shown him? "

" Yes," he said.

" But," I said, " if someone were to drag him out up the steep and rugged ascent, and did not let go till he had been dragged up to the light of the sun, would not his forced journey be one of pain and annoyance, and when he came to the light, would not his eyes be so full of the glare that he would not be able to see a single one of the objects we now call true? "

" Certainly not all at once," he said.

" Yes, I fancy that he would need time before he could see things in the world above. At first he would most easily see shadows, then the reflection in water of men and everything else, and, finally, the things themselves. After that he could look at the heavenly bodies and the sky itself by night, turning his eyes to the light of the stars and the moon more easily than to the sun and the sun's light by day? "

" Surely."

" Then last of all, I fancy, he would be able to look at the sun and observe its nature, not its appearance in water or on alien material, but the very sun itself in its own place."

.   .   .   .   .   .

" Well, then, if he is reminded of his original abode and its wisdom, and those who were then his fellow-prisoners, do you not think that he will pity them and count himself happy in the change? "

" Certainly."

" Now, suppose that those prisoners had had among themselves a system of honours and commendations; that prizes were granted to the man who had the keenest eye for passing objects and the best memory for which usually came first, and which second, and which came together, and who could most cleverly conjecture from this what was likely to come in the future; do you think that our friend would think longingly of those prizes and envy the men whom the prisoners honour and set in authority? Would he not rather feel what Homer described, and—wish earnestly

> To live on earth a swain
> Or serve a swain for hire,

or suffer anything rather than be so the victim of seeming and live in their way?"

"Yes," he said, "I certainly think that he would endure anything rather than that."

"Then consider this point," I said. "If this man were to descend again and take his seat in his old place, would not his eyes be full of darkness because he had just come out of the sunlight?"

"Most certainly," he said.

"And suppose that he had again to take part with the prisoners there in the old contest of distinguishing between the shadows, while his sight was confused and before his eyes had got steady (and it might take them quite a considerable time to get used to the darkness), would not men laugh at him, and say that having gone up above he had come back with his sight ruined, so that it was not worth while even to try to go up? And do you not think that they would kill him who tried to release them and bear them up, if they could lay hands on him, and slay him?"

"Certainly," he said.

"Now this simile, my dear Glaucon, must be applied in all its parts to what we said before; the sphere revealed by sight being likened to the prison dwelling, and the light of the fire therein to the power of the sun. If you will set the upward ascent and the seeing of the things in the upper world with the upward journey of the soul to the intelligible sphere, you will have my surmise; and that is what you are anxious to have. Whether it be actually true, God knows. But this is how it appears to me. In the world of knowledge the Form of the good is perceived last and with difficulty, but when it is seen it must be inferred that it is the cause of all that is right and beautiful in all things, producing in the visible world light and the lord of light, and being itself lord in the intelligible world and the giver of truth and reason, and this Form of the good must be seen by whosoever would act wisely in public or in private."

" I agree with you," he said, " so far as I am capable."

" Come then," I said, "and agree with me in this also; and don't be surprised that they who have come thus far are unwilling to trouble themselves with mortal affairs, and that their souls are ever eager to dwell above. For this is but natural if the image we have related is true."

" It is," he said.

" Then do you think it at all surprising," I said, " if one who has come from divine visions to the world of men plays a sorry part and appears very ridiculous when, with eyes still confused and before he has got properly used to the darkness that is round him, he is compelled to contend in law courts or elsewhere concerning the shadows of the just or the images which throw those shadows, or to dispute concerning the manner in which those images are conceived by men who have never seen real justice ? "

" No, it is anything but surprising," he said.

" Yes," I said, " a sensible man would remember that the eyes may be confused in two ways, and for two reasons—by a change from light to darkness, or from darkness to light. He will consider that the same may happen with the soul,

and when he sees a soul in trouble and unable to perceive,
he will not laugh without thinking; rather he will examine
whether it has come from a brighter light and is dim because
it is not accustomed to the darkness, or whether it is on its
way from ignorance to greater brightness and is dazzled
with the greater brilliance; and so he will count the first
happy in its condition and its life, but the second he will
pity, and if he please to laugh at it, his laughter will be less
ridiculous than that of him who laughs at the soul that has
come from the light above."   A. D. LINDSAY.

THEAETETUS

The Portrait of the Philosopher as contrasted with the Man of the World

THEAETETUS 172. Text: Lewis Campbell's Edition. Translation:
B. Jowett.

(In the course of a digression in this dialogue (the main subject
of which is the nature of knowledge) Socrates expatiates on
the freedom of the philosophic life, removed by the all-absorbing
interest in truth from the temptations to follow the ordinary objects
of pursuit and flatter those in power. The portrait is that of the
"spectator of all time and all existence," in the ordinary state, in
which he must hold aloof from politics, since he cannot reform
them. It may be taken as a companion to that of the philosopher
in the *Republic*, who devotes his highest powers to the service of
the state which has educated him. It gives us an expression of
that freedom of the mind which was a necessary condition of the
good life for Plato and Aristotle. Certain touches also illustrate
the peculiar Greek notion contained in the untranslatable word
"Banausia," the idea of an illiberalism or narrowness of mind and
temperament resulting from any excessive specialisation, whether
in physical or mental labour. In reading the somewhat bitter
description of the lawyer, we must bear in mind the character of
the Athenian law courts, the appeals to popular passion motived by
the numbers and often ignorance of the judges (*dikasts*), and how
all this had been burnt into Plato's experience in the trial of Socrates;
but of course Plato's lawyer is a type representing tendencies of
human nature which are always with us.)

Socrates. Those who have passed their days in the pursuit
of philosophy are ridiculously at fault when they have to
appear and speak in court. How natural this is!

Theodorus. What do you mean?

Socrates. I mean to say that those who have been trained in philosophy and liberal pursuits are as unlike those who from their youth upwards have been knocking about in the courts and such places as a freeman is in breeding unlike a slave.

Theodorus. In what is the difference seen?

Socrates. In the leisure which a freeman can always command: he has his talk out in peace, and like ourselves, he wanders at will from one subject to another, and from a second to a third,—if the fancy takes him, he begins again, as we are doing now, caring not whether his words are many or few; his only aim is to attain the truth. But the lawyer is always in a hurry; there is the water of the clepsydra driving him on and not allowing him to expatiate at will: and there is his adversary standing over him, enforcing his rights; the indictment which in their phraseology is termed the affidavit, is recited at the time: and from this he must not deviate. He is a servant and is always disputing about a fellow-servant before his master, who is seated and has the cause in his hands; the trial is never about some indifferent matter, but always concerns himself; and often the race is for his life. The consequence has been, that he has become keen and shrewd; he has learned how to flatter his master in word and indulge him in deed; but his soul is small and unrighteous. His condition, which has been that of a slave from his youth upwards, has deprived him of growth and uprightness, and independence; dangers and fears which were too much for his truth and honesty, came upon him in early years, when the tenderness of youth was unequal to them, and he has been driven into crooked ways; from the first he has practised deception and retaliation, and has become stunted and warped. And so he has passed out of youth into manhood having no soundness in him, and is now, as he thinks, a master in wisdom. Such is the lawyer, Theodorus.

Will you have the companion picture of the philosopher, who is of our brotherhood?

. . . . . .

173.

I will describe, then, the leaders, for there is no use in talking about the inferior sort. In the first place, the lords of philosophy have never from their youth upwards known their way to the Agora, or the dicastery, or the council, or any other political assembly; they neither see nor hear the laws or the decrees of the state written or recited; the eagerness of political societies in the attainment of offices—clubs and banquets, and revels and singing maidens, do not enter even into their dreams. Whether any event has turned out well or ill in the city, what disgrace may have descended to anyone from his ancestors, male or female, are matters of which the philosopher no more knows than he can tell, as they say, how many pints are contained in the ocean. Neither is he conscious of his ignorance. For he does not hold aloof in order that he may gain a reputation, but the truth is that the outer form of him only is in the city; his mind disdaining the littlenesses and nothingnesses of human things, is " flying all abroad," as Pindar says, measuring earth and heaven and the things which are under and on the earth and above the heaven, interrogating the whole nature of each and all in their entirety, but not condescending to anything which is within reach.

Theodorus. What do you mean, Socrates?

Socrates. I will illustrate my meaning, Theodorus, by the jest which the clever, witty Thracian handmaid is said to have made about Thales, when he fell into a well, as he was looking up at the stars. She said that he was so eager to know what was going on in heaven, that he could not see what was before his feet. This is a jest which is equally applicable to all philosophers. For the philosopher is wholly

L

unacquainted with his next-door neighbour; he is ignorant, not only of what he is doing, but he hardly knows whether he is a man or an animal; he is searching into the essence of man, and busy in enquiring what belongs to such a nature to do or suffer different from any other;—I think that you understand me, Theodorus?

Theodorus. I do, and what you say is true.

Socrates. And thus, my friend, on every occasion, private as well as public, as I said at first, when he appears in a law court or in any place in which he has to speak of things which are at his feet and before his eyes, he is the jest, not only of Thracian handmaids but of the general herd, tumbling into wells and every sort of disaster through his inexperience. His awkwardness is fearful, and gives the impression of imbecility. When he is reviled, he has nothing personal to say in answer to the civilities of his adversaries, for he knows no scandals of anyone, and they do not interest him; and therefore he is laughed at for his sheepishness; and when others are being praised and glorified, in the simplicity of his heart, he cannot help going into fits of laughter, so that he seems to be a downright idiot. When he hears a tyrant or a king eulogised, he fancies that he is listening to the praises of some keeper of cattle—a swineherd or shepherd, or perhaps a cowherd, who is congratulated on the quantity of milk which he squeezes from them, and he remarks that the creature whom they tend, and out of whom they squeeze the wealth, is of a less tractable and more insidious nature. Then, again, he observes that the great man is of necessity as ill-mannered and uneducated as any shepherd—for he has no leisure, and he is surrounded by a wall, which is his mountain-pen. Hearing of enormous landed proprietors of ten thousand acres and more, our philosopher deems this to be a trifle, because he had been accustomed to think of the whole earth; and when they sing the praises of family and say that someone is a gentleman because he can show seven generations of wealthy ancestors, he thinks that their sentiments only betray a dull and narrow vision in those who utter them, and who are not educated enough to look at the whole, nor to consider that every man has had thousands and ten thousand of progenitors, and among them have been rich and poor, kings and slaves, Hellenes and barbarians innumerable. And when people pride themselves on having a pedigree of twenty-five ancestors which goes back to Amphitryon, he cannot understand their poverty of ideas. Why are they unable to calculate that Amphitryon had a twenty-fifth ancestor who might have been anybody and was such as fortune made him, and he had a fiftieth and so on? He amuses himself with the notion that they cannot count, and thinks that a little arithmetic would have got rid of their senseless vanity. Now in all these cases our philosopher is derided by the vulgar, partly because he is thought to despise them, and also because he is ignorant of what is before him, and always at a loss.

Theodorus. That is very true, Socrates.

Socrates. But O, my friend, when he draws the other into upper air and gets him out of his pleas and rejoinders into the contemplation of justice and injustice in their own nature, and in their difference from one another and all other things; or from the commonplaces about the happiness of a king or of a rich man to the consideration of government, and of human happiness and misery in general— what they are, and how a man is to attain the one and avoid the other—when that narrow, keen, little legal mind is called to account about all this, he gives the philosopher his revenge; for dizzied by the height at which he is hanging, whence he looks down into space, which is a strange experience to him, he being dismayed and lost, and stammering broken words, is laughed at, not by Thracian handmaidens or any other uneducated persons, for they have no eye for the situation, but by every man who had not been brought up a slave. Such are the two characters, Theodorus, the one of the freeman who has been trained in liberty and leisure, whom you call the philosopher—him we cannot blame because he appears simple and is of no account when he has to perform some menial task. . . . The other character is that of the man who is able to do all this kind of service smartly and neatly, but knows not how with the music of discourse to hymn the true life aright which is lived by immortals or men blessed of heaven.

Theodorus. If you could only persuade everybody, Socrates, as you do me, of the truth of your words, there would be more peace and fewer evils among men.

Socrates. Evils, Theodorus, can never pass away; for there must always remain something which is antagonistic to good.

B. JOWETT.

PHILEBUS

Text: R. G. Bury's Edition. Translation: B. Jowett. Plato's dialogue *Philebus* treats ethical questions in a way which is at times very abstract and metaphysical. It seems to breathe an atmosphere far from the struggle and strain after righteousness which pervades the *Republic*. It calmly contemplates human life as a work of art which can be made beautiful by infusing as much harmony and symmetry into it as possible. It is concentrated upon the one question—What are the elements of the ideal life; in what proportion should they be combined, if human existence is to reflect the eternal good and beauty? We are in a rare atmosphere where conflict is hardly admitted, and the true Platonic principle of measure, harmony, the finite regulating the formless, is supreme. The original question is whether the good for man is to be found more in the life of pleasure, or that of wisdom. The extracts illustrate the point of view of the dialogue, though not presenting fully the complex argument.

Is Pleasure the Good or Wisdom?

20.

Socrates. Is the good perfect or imperfect?

Protarchus. The most perfect, Socrates, of all things.

Socrates. And is the good sufficient?

Protarchus. Yes, certainly, and in a degree surpassing all other things.

Socrates. And no one can deny that all percipient beings desire and hunt after the good, and are eager to catch and have the good about them, and care not for the attainment of anything which is not accompanied by good.

Protarchus. That is undeniable.

Socrates. Now let us part off the life of pleasure from the life of wisdom, and pass them in review.

Protarchus. How do you mean?

Socrates. Let there be no wisdom in the life of pleasure, nor any pleasure in the life of wisdom, for if either of them is the chief good, it cannot be supposed to want anything; but if either is supposed to want anything, then it cannot really be the chief good.

Protarchus. Impossible.

Socrates. And will you help us to test these two lives?

Protarchus. Certainly.

Socrates. Then answer. Would you choose, Protarchus, to live all your life long in the enjoyment of the greatest pleasures?

Protarchus. Certainly, I should.

Socrates. Would you consider that there was still anything wanting to you, if you had perfect pleasure?

Protarchus. Certainly not.

Socrates. Reflect, would you not want wisdom and intelligence and forethought, and similar qualities? Would you not at any rate want sight?

Protarchus. Why should I? Having pleasure I should have all things.

Socrates. Living thus you would always throughout your life enjoy the greatest pleasures?

Protarchus. I should.

Socrates. But if you had neither mind, nor memory, nor knowledge, nor true opinion, you would in the first place be utterly ignorant of whether you were pleased or not, because you would be entirely devoid of intelligence.

Protarchus. Certainly.

Socrates. And similarly, if you had no memory you would not recollect that you had ever been pleased, nor would the slightest recollection of the pleasure which you feel at any moment remain with you; and if you had no true opinion you would not think that you were pleased when you were; and if you had no power of calculation you would not be able to calculate on future pleasure, and your life would be the life, not of a man, but of an oyster or " pulmo marinus." Could this be otherwise?

Protarchus. No.

Socrates. But is such a life eligible?

Protarchus. I cannot answer you, Socrates; the argument has taken away from me the power of speech.

Socrates. We must keep up our spirits; let us now take the life of mind and examine it in turn.

Protarchus. And what is this life of mind?

Socrates. I want to know whether anyone of us would consent to live having wisdom, and mind and knowledge and memory of all things, but having no sense of pleasure or pain, and wholly unaffected by these and the like feelings?

Protarchus. Neither life, Socrates, appears eligible to me, nor is likely, as I should imagine, to be chosen by anyone else.

Socrates. What would you say, Protarchus, to both of these, in one or to one that was made out of the union of the two?

Protarchus. Out of the union, that is, of pleasure with mind and wisdom?

Socrates. Yes, that is the life which I mean.

Protarchus. There can be no difference of opinion; not

some but all would surely choose this third rather than either of the other two, and in addition to them.

Socrates. But do you see the consequences?

Protarchus. To be sure I do. The consequence is that two out of the three lives which have been proposed are neither sufficient nor eligible for man or for animal. . . .

Socrates. And now have I not sufficiently shown that Philebus' goddess is not to be regarded as identical with the good?

Philebus. Neither is your " mind " the good, Socrates, for that will be open to the same objection.

Socrates. Perhaps you may be right, Philebus, in saying so of my " mind," but of the true which is also the divine mind, far otherwise.

The Universe ordered by Mind

28.

Socrates. Let us begin, Protarchus, by asking a question. Whether all this which they call the Universe is left to the guidance of unreason and chance medley, or on the contrary, as our fathers have declared, ordered and governed by a marvellous intelligence and wisdom?

Protarchus. Wide asunder are the two assertions, illustrious Socrates, for that which you were just now saying appears to be blasphemy; but the other assertion, that mind orders all things, is worthy of the aspect of the world, and of the sun, and of the moon, and of the stars, and of the whole circle of the heavens; and never will I say or think otherwise.

Socrates. Shall we then agree with them of old time in maintaining this doctrine—not merely reasserting the notions of others without risk to ourselves—but shall we share in the danger, and take our part of the reproach which will await us, when an ingenious individual declares that all is disorder?

Protarchus. That would certainly be my wish.

The Principles which make Life Good

64.

Socrates. May we not say with reason that we are now at the vestibule of the habitation of the good?

Protarchus. I think that we are.

Socrates. What, then, is there in the mixture which is most precious, and which is the principal cause why such a state is universally beloved by all? When we have discovered it, we will proceed to ask whether this omnipresent nature is more akin to pleasure or to mind.

Protarchus. Quite right; in that way we shall be better able to judge.

Socrates. And there is no difficulty in seeing the cause which renders any mixture either of the highest value or of none at all.

Protarchus. What do you mean?

Socrates. Every man knows it.

Protarchus. What?

Socrates. He knows that any want of measure and symmetry in any mixture whatever must of necessity be fatal both to the elements and to the mixture which is then not a mixture, but only a confused medley which brings confusion on the possessor of it.

Protarchus. Most true.

Socrates. And now the power of the good has retired into the region of the beautiful, for measure and symmetry are beauty and virtue all the world over.

Protarchus. True.

Socrates. And we also said that truth was to form an element in the mixture.

Protarchus. Certainly.

Socrates. Then if we are not able to hunt the good with one idea only, with three we may catch our prey; Beauty, Symmetry, Truth are the three, and these taken together we may regard as the single cause of the mixture, and the mixture as being good by reason of the infusion of them.

Protarchus. Quite right.

Socrates. And now, Protarchus, any man could decide well enough whether wisdom is more akin to the highest good and more honourable among gods and men.

B. Jowett.

(In the application with which the dialogue concludes to the good things which are to be mixed in human life, there are admitted after measure, beauty and symmetry, mind and wisdom, the sciences and arts, and the pure pleasures of the soul, and of the senses of sight and hearing. Thus Plato includes the purest pleasures, but only gives them a subordinate place.)

LAWS

Text: E. B. England's Edition, with notes. The *Laws*, a dialogue in ten books, thought to be composed of writings of Plato's old age, appears to convey the thoughts and teaching on politics and morals which he was most anxious to leave to his countrymen as a result of his experience and reflection on human life. The high and idealistic enthusiasm of the *Republic* is almost gone, but the work is a mine of profound observations on human character, the universal tendencies of men and women, and their response to circumstances and diverse influences. On all Plato's more serious views there is, so to speak, a heavier stamp, and they leave a still deeper impression on our minds, as, for example, the doctrine that no man does evil willingly. Lofty passages of speculation occur, such as that on the origins of civilised states (from which the first extract is taken), and on the existence of God and other divine powers, and the relation of man to the Universe, a short extract from which is the last quotation.

Advance in Civilisation brings Increase of Vice as well as of Virtue

Laws iii. 676. The speakers are an Athenian stranger, Cleinias a Cretan, and Megillus a Lacedaemonian—and the main subject of their discussion the foundation of a new Cretan colony and the best legislation for it. The Athenian is the chief speaker, and the dialogue often tends to become a monologue.

.   .   .   .

Athenian. What shall we say to have been the beginning of civil government? Should we not be likely to discover this most speedily and successfully starting from the point from which we can observe the progress of states, advancing severally towards virtue or towards vice?

Cleinias. What point do you mean?

Athenian. From a consideration I think of the infinite length of time, and the changes that take place in it.

Cleinias. What exactly have you in mind?

Athenian. Well, do you suppose that you have ever reflected how great a period of time has elapsed since cities have existed, and men lived in states?

Cleinias. Certainly that is by no means easy.

Athenian. It may be regarded as immeasurable and inconceivable?

Cleinias. Assuredly it is that.

Athenian. Have not myriads on myriads of cities come into being in this time, and whatever the number, not less been destroyed, and have they not tried all kinds of constitutions severally many times over, and at times have passed from less to greater, and again from greater to less, and from better have become worse, and from worse better?

Cleinias. Necessarily so.

Athenian. Let us then grasp, if we can, the cause of this process of change, for perhaps this would reveal to us the secret of the birth and change of states.

Cleinias. You say well, and it behoves us to give all our minds to the quest—you in unfolding your view on these problems; us in following you closely.

Athenian. Shall we then assume that there is some truth in the ancient legends?

Cleinias. Of which sort?

Athenian. In regard to the many destructions of men which have occurred, through floods and diseases, and many other disasters in which only a small part of the human race survived.

Cleinias. Anyone may accept as very probable any story of that kind.

Athenian. Let us then suppose out of the many, one particular destruction to have once happened by flood.

Cleinias. In what way are we to think about it?

Athenian. That those who then escaped the destruction were mountain herdsmen; on mountain peaks were preserved the few sparks for the lighting again of the human race.

Cleinias. Evidently.

Athenian. Of course such men would be inexperienced both in the other arts and in all the tricks devised by city-dwellers to overreach and contend in rivalry, and in other ways wrong each other.

Cleinias. That is likely enough.

Athenian. Shall we assume the cities in the plains and situated by the sea to have been utterly destroyed at that time?

Cleinias. Let us assume this.

. . . . . .

678.

Athenian. Now do you suppose that there would be any remembrance at all, so to speak, of city and constitution and legislation, which is the subject of our present discourse?

Cleinias. None at all.

Athenian. Is it not then out of such conditions as these that our whole civilisation of to-day has developed, cities and constitutions, and arts, and laws, and much wickedness; also much virtue?

Cleinias. How do you mean?

Athenian. Do you think, my dear fellow, that the men of that time, inexperienced as they were both in much that is valuable in city life and in much that is the opposite, would have reached a high degree either of virtue or of vice?

Cleinias. You say well, and I understand what you mean.

Athenian. But with the progress of time and multiplica-

tion of the human race, all things have advanced to their
present condition?

Cleinias. Very true.

Athenian. In all probability, however, not suddenly but
little by little in the course of immense ages.

.   .   .   .   .   .

Athenian. In addition to the lack of the arts, all those that
are dependent on iron and brass and all metals of this kind,
yet more would have vanished at that epoch.

Cleinias. To what do you refer?

Athenian. Why faction, together with war, would be
everywhere done away with at that time.

Cleinias. Why so?

Athenian. In the first place, because they had friendly
feelings and kindly affection for one another on account
of their isolation; secondly, because they had not to con-
679 tend for the means of subsistence. For there was no lack of
pasture, except perhaps for some among them, at the
beginning, and this constituted their greatest source of
support at that time. For they were never in lack of milk
and of meat; by hunting, also, they secured a plentiful supply
of food, not to be despised.

.   .   .   .

679b.

On this account they were in no great poverty, nor forced
by poverty to become hostile to each other. And rich they
who were without gold and silver would never be, and this
was then their condition. And in any association whatever,
in which neither wealth nor poverty is a member, in this the
best customs grow up. For there neither insolence, nor wrong,
nor jealousies and envies are fostered. For these reasons
and on account of what is called simplicity, they were good.
When they heard anything called noble or base, they supposed in their simplicity that this was rightly named, and

believed it. No one knew so much as to suspect a lie through cleverness, as we do now. What they were told about Gods and men, they held to be true and lived accordingly. Wherefore they were in every respect such as we have just described them.

Cleinias. In my opinion these things were entirely as you say.

God the Measure of All Things

LAWS iv. 716c. Plato here gives a striking expression to the doctrine which pervades so much of his philosophy that the principle of measure, or harmony, is the cause of all that is good in the world and human life, by reminding us that God, the principle in its divine aspect, is also the measure in the sense of determining what the world is for all minds that know it. Thus he makes a sublime correction of the saying of the Sophist Protagoras that "man is the measure of all things," a statement which would signify the relativity of knowledge to the individual consciousness, as also of the judgment of good and evil.

. . . . .

Athenian. What kind of action is dear to God and follows God? There is only one and it finds its one expression in the old saying that like will love like when it is according to measure, for things that know no measure love neither each other nor those that do. Now God is for us in the highest sense the measure of all things, much rather than is, as some say, man individual the measure. He then who would become friend to such an one must to the utmost of his power, as far as possible, himself be of this character. And on this principle the man among us who is temperate, is a friend to God, for he is like Him, but the intemperate unlike and different, and with the unjust and those with other vices, the same holds good. Let us consider the principle which naturally follows and is in my judgment of all principles the most beautiful and true; that to the good man it is noblest and best and most helpful to the blessed life ever to sacrifice, and hold communion with the Gods, with prayers,

offerings, and every kind of service. This is more than aught
else seemly for the good, but to the wicked in every way
contrary.

.   .   .   .   .   .

Honour to Parents

(After regulations for the service of the Gods and honours to
Heroes.)

717b.

Next in order come honours to living parents. Those
to whom one owes the first and greatest of debts, one ought
as a sacred duty to repay with the most exalted honours,
and to consider that all that one has and holds belong to
those who gave him birth and nurture, so that he is bound
to make his all minister to their service to the utmost of his
capacity, including his substance, and powers of body and mind,
and thereby repay the debt of cares and pains which they
have bestowed on him—an expenditure made of old for him
in youth, and which, moreover, the son repays to the old
when age has brought them to need. Throughout life he
ought to have held and to hold to his parents the gentlest
speech, for very heavy is the penalty for careless and winged
words, and as a watcher in these matters over all men is
set Nemesis, the messenger of justice. Therefore a son
should bow before a parent's anger, even when vented in
resentful word or deed, and should make allowance for the
special provocation there must be in the mere thought that
one's son should have done the wrong.

.   .   .   .   .   .

The Honour due to the Soul

Laws v. 726. Plato's treatment of the conditions of the good life
as organised by the law-giver, and also by the influence of moral
approval and disapproval.
The standpoint is rather more subjective than that of the *Republic*.

Plato considers the moral life as the life in which the noblest part
of the individual—the soul—is honoured, and treats of love of self
as the source of all evil. But the emphasis on the laws of the city
as giving infallible standards of conduct is strange to us, unless we
remember that Plato conceives the possibility of raising his legislators above human weaknesses, even though the legislators of
the *Laws* are not the perfect philosophers of the *Republic*.

　　　　　·　　　·　　　·　　　·

Athenian. Of all that enters into the world of man, after
the Gods, the soul being nearest to him is most divine. Now
the things which are our own are of two kinds. Those that
are superior in power and nobility are the ruling elements;
those that are weaker and inferior, the subservient. Therefore
the parts of himself that rule should always be held in honour
727 above those that serve. Wherefore it is right that I ordain
that after the Gods who rule and those who come next to
these in pre-eminence, we honour in the second place our
own soul. But none of us so to speak rightly honours the soul,
though we seem to do so. For honour is a divine good, of
harmful things none is esteemed honourable. He who thinks
to exalt his soul with words, or gifts or compliance, without
bringing it from a worse to a better state, seems indeed to
honour it, but does so in no sense at all. Everyone straightway from boyhood supposes himself capable of knowing
everything and thinks to honour his soul by praising it, and
eagerly encourages it to do whatever it desires. According
to our present discourse, this is to injure it and not to
reverence. And reverence, we say, ought to be given to it,
in the second place, after the Gods. Neither when a man
does not on every occasion suppose himself to be the cause
of his own errors—yea of the majority and greatest of his
evils—but blames others, and ever puffs himself up as not
responsible, though he supposes himself to be honouring his
own soul, does he so; rather is he far from it. For he does
it a hurt. Nor when against the advice and approval of the
law-giver he indulges it with pleasure, does he in any way

bestow honour on it but dishonour, filling it with evils and change of purpose. Again when, on the other hand, he does not learn steadfastness by toiling at the labours and enduring the terrors and griefs and pains, commended to him by the law, but succumbs, neither then in giving way does he honour the soul. In all these ways he dishonours it. Nor when he conceives of life as in all circumstances a good does he honour, but there again dishonours it. For the soul supposing the hereafter to be altogether evil, he gives way to this thought and does not resist it by teaching and disproving, as if not knowing that the opposite may be the truth, and the kingdom of the Gods below the greatest of all goods for us. Neither when anyone prefers physical beauty to virtue, is this anything but the real and total dishonour of the soul. This conception falsely argues the body to be more honourable than the soul. For nothing that is earth-born is more honourable than the heavenly, and he who thinks otherwise concerning the soul knows not what a marvellous pos-
728 session he is neglecting. Neither when a man delights in the possession of ill-gotten gains, or does not feel distress at their possession, does he then honour his soul with gifts, but on the contrary is as far from it as possible. For that which is precious and lovely in himself he gives away for a small amount of gold. For all the gold both above and under the earth is not to be offered in exchange for virtue. To sum up the matter, he who is unwilling to withhold himself by every means from those practices which the law-giver may severally declare to be base and evil, and to devote himself with all his power to those which on the contrary he declares good and noble, this man whoever he be is, without knowing it, bringing hideous disgrace upon the majesty of his soul. The so-called just meed of ill-doing, the greatest there is, no one so to speak takes into account. The greatest penalty is to grow like the men who are vicious, and to flee and be

severed from good men and principles, and to cleave to the bad, mingling with their company. When one attaches himself to such men, of necessity he does and tolerates what they are accustomed to in behaviour and converse. This state of his, then, has nothing just in it as the word "justice" or punishment suggests, for justice and a just verdict is something fair, but it is retribution, the state which follows injustice. And both he who meets with it, and he who does not, are alike wretched, for the former is not cured, whilst the latter is lost so that many may be saved. In short, it may be said that our glory lies in following the better, and as for the worse, where they are capable of improvement, to do our utmost to bring this to pass.

There is surely nothing that a man possesses more fitted than the soul for the avoidance of evil, the discernment and choice of the supremely best, and having made the choice to dwell together with it for the rest of life. Therefore the second place was assigned to it in the order of value. The third, as everyone would agree, would be naturally given to the body. We ought therefore to consider the honours belonging to it, and of these which are the true and how many spurious. The law-giver declares them, as it seems to me, as follows. The body is honourable, not because of beauty or strength, or swiftness or size, nor even for health, though this is the view of many, nor indeed for the opposite qualities, but those bodies which possess all these properties in a moderate degree have by far the most temperate and the safest constitution. As for the extremes, the one makes the souls boastful and overbold, the other depressed and illiberal. Similarly with the possession of money and goods, it falls 729 under the same scale of values. The possession of these in excess causes hatreds and seditions in states; the lack of them usually servitude. Let not anyone love the heaping up of money for the sake of his children, so that he may leave

M

them as rich as possible. For this is not a blessing either for them or the city. For the young, a competence not attractive to flattery, whilst not lacking in the necessities of life, is of all things the most favourable to culture and the best. For this being in harmony with our nature, and suitable in all respects, constitutes a life free from pain. To children we should bequeath not gold but the spirit of reverence. But we suppose that we shall secure this for them by scolding those who are shameless. This, however, does not come about from our present exhortation, when we insist that youth should be respectful in all ways. The wise legislator would rather counsel the elders to have reverence for the young, and above all to beware lest any youth should either see or hear him doing or saying anything base, inasmuch as where the old are without shame, it is inevitable that the young be most shameless. For the education of the young, and at the same time of themselves, lies essentially—not in admonition —but in this, that he who exhorts another in any way should be seen himself to follow throughout life what he teaches.

He, moreover, who honours and reverences the family bond, and all the members who share the worship of the family gods, having the same blood in their veins, he will, as seems right, have the gods propitious in his offspring. And the man who esteems the services of his friends and comrades to himself as greater and more valuable than they do, and his own kindnesses to his friends and comrades less than they esteem them, will possess in the intercourse of life friends and comrades of goodwill. And both in relation to his city and the citizens, by far the best is that man who would place before an Olympian victory and all contests both of war and peace, the fame of obedience to his native laws, as of all men most distinguished through life in their service. In relation to strangers, it must be recognised that contracts have a special sacredness. For almost all the concerns of strangers are the care of God, and offences against strangers beyond those against citizens have God for their avenger, for the stranger, since he lacks comrades and relations, is more piteous before men and Gods. He, then, who has greater power of vengeance has the greater will to succour, and the guardian spirit of each stranger is powerful in the highest degree and is minister of Zeus, the protector of 730 strangers. Let him, then, who has even a little forethought have a care that he pass through life to the end committing no offence against strangers. But of all offences, both against strangers and against citizens, greatest in every case is that which is committed against suppliants. For God whom the suppliant had as witness when he failed to secure a promise of safety becomes the greatest protector of the sufferer, so that he who thus suffered would never remain unavenged.

.   .   .   .   .   .

In what follows we shall consider the character of that man who is to pass his life in the noblest way, the matters which must now be determined concerning that sphere in which it is not law but education of individuals by praise and blame, which makes them docile and well-disposed to those whose task it is to legislate.

Now truth is the greatest of all goods for Gods and men. He who looks to be blest and happy should from the first be a partner in truth so that he may live as a man of truth for the longest possible time. For he is worthy of trust. But he is untrustworthy who willingly holds falsehood dear, and if unwillingly, he is a fool, and neither of these is enviable. For friendless are they all, both the untrustworthy and the stupid. And as time passes, the untrustworthy man being known for such prepares for himself in a difficult old age, complete solitude at the end of life, so that whether his associates and children are alive or dead, almost equally his life becomes bereaved. He again who never does a wrong is honourable, but the man who does not even suffer the wrong-doers to wrong, deserves honour more than double the first. For the former counts as one in value, the latter is equivalent to many, since he gives information to the authorities of the wrong-doing of others. And he who co-operates with all his might with the rulers in their chastise-ments, the great and perfect citizen, let him be proclaimed to carry off the victory in virtue. The same praise it is fitting to give to temperance and wisdom, and all those other goods such that their possessor is able not only to have them himself, but to impart them to others.

.   .   .   .   .   .

731b.

Courageous should every man be, and gentle as far as in him lies. For the crimes of others which are difficult and hard to cure, or even altogether incurable, cannot be other-wise avoided than by contending, defending, winning the victory, and inflexibly punishing, and this the soul is quite unable to do without a righteous indignation. But in regard to those sins which are committed but are curable, it must first be recognised that no wrong-doer does wrong willingly. For no one ever willingly possessed any of the greatest evils, least of all in the most precious part of himself. And the soul, as we say, is in reality the most precious part of all. No one, then, would willingly ever take to himself in the most excel-lent part the greatest evil, and live through life in the pos-session of it. But the unjust man, and he who possesses evil things, is in every way worthy of pity. It is permissible, then, to pity one who is incurable, and restraining our anger deal gently with him, not storming like an angry woman. But on those who are unrestrainedly and incorrigibly disorderly and vicious, we ought to let loose our indignation. Hence, it beseems the good man to be both capable of anger and of mildness, according to the occasion.

But the greatest of all evils for the majority of human beings is one that is inborn in the soul. And since everyone pardons himself for this, he does not devise any way of escape. This is what they mean when they say that man is by nature a friend to himself, and rightly so, for such he ought to be. But the truth is that the cause of all sins for everyone in every case is this, the too great love of self. For the lover is blind in regard to his beloved, so that he is a bad judge of what is right and good and noble, always thinking that what concerns himself must be honoured before the truth.

732b.

But he who would be great ought not to cherish himself nor his own interests, but what is just, whether it happen to be done by himself or rather by another. From this same error also has arisen in all minds the folly of supposing that wisdom lies in oneself. Hence when we know, so to speak, nothing, we think we know everything, and instead of entrusting to others the things we do not know how to do, we ourselves are driven to do them wrong.

Wherefore every man should avoid this too great love of self and follow the man who is better than himself, thinking it no shame to prefer such an one.

Great Wealth and Goodness Incompatible

LAWS v. 742d.

Now the aim of the wise statesman is not, we say, that which according to the multitude the good legislator ought to desire; that the state for which he legislates wisely should be the greatest possible, and the wealthiest, possessing gold and silver and having sway by land and sea to the greatest extent. They may add, indeed, to this that he who legislates aright ought to endeavour that the state should be most virtuous and most happy. Of these things, some are possible and some are not. Those that are possible the law-giver will wish to achieve; he will send no vain wishes in the direction of the impossible, neither will he attempt it. For true well-being and goodness almost of necessity coincide. At this, then, he would aim. But to be very rich and also good is impossible; in the sense I mean in which the majority reckon people rich. For they call rich those (of whom there are few) whose possessions have the largest money-value, and this is what a bad man might acquire. And if this is so, I, for my part, could never concede to them that the rich man can have true happiness, not being also good. And to excel in goodness and in wealth is impossible.

(In the explanation of this which follows, Plato argues that while the acquisitions which proceed from just transactions only are less than half in value those which result from transactions both just and unjust, those who spend on noble as well as necessary objects, spend twice as much as those whose expenditure is on necessary objects only. And as it is the man who has only used just methods of acquisition who will give half his substance to noble or perhaps, we may say, philanthropic objects, he, the good man, can never be wealthy.)

.   .   .   .   .   .

The Place of Man in the Universal Order

LAWS x. 903. In Plato we have the greatest expression in Ancient Greek thought of that interpretation of human life which has been so philosophically attractive to some of the deepest thinkers, and so full of consolation to many unable to see any other solution of the problem of evil. Man and his experience, being a fragmentary part of a vast and perfect whole, are necessarily unintelligible, unless viewed in relation to that whole, nor can the individual hope fully to perceive the meaning of his own existence, since he cannot perceive the All. The following passage only expresses in part what is the spirit of a good deal of Plato's philosophy, though it must not be forgotten that he admits at times a principle intractable to good.

Athenian. I think we have now sufficiently reasoned with the man who accuses the Gods of neglect.

Cleinias. We have.

Athenian. Compelled by our logic, he admits that he was wrong. He seems to me, however, to be in need also of the persuasive charm of an appeal to his imagination.

Cleinias. Of what kind, my friend?

Athenian. We must persuade the youth by our arguments that all things have been fitted together by him who has care of all with a view to the preservation and excellence of the whole, the parts of which, each according to its capacity, suffer and do what is fitting for them. For each of these arrangements, even to the minutest experience and act, there are appointed controllers who have achieved perfection in the minutest details. Of these thy one small portion, O pitiful man, ever looking to the whole, tends to this, very small though it be. But thou art ignorant in regard to this very thing that the whole of creation comes to be for this end, that the life of the All should be blessed, and that the process of the universe is not on thy account but thou for the sake of the universe. For every physician and every skilful worker works throughout for the sake of the whole, directing his efforts to the common good; he completes the part for the sake of the whole, and not the whole for the sake of the part. But thou art discontented, being ignorant how what befalls thee is best for the universe, and for thee also in virtue of the power of thy common origin. Since the soul attached to a body, now one, now another, suffers all kinds of changes, occasioned either by itself or by another soul, no other task remains for Him who moves the pieces on the draught-board but to transfer the character which has become better to a better sphere, that which has deteriorated to a worse, according to what is suitable for each, in order that each may obtain as his lot the destiny which beseems him.

ARISTOTLE

384–322 B.C.

Born at Stagira, in Thrace, he was a student in Plato's Academy from 367 B.C. to Plato's death in 347 B.C. He was tutor to Alexander of Macedon, 343–340 B.C. After Alexander's accession he founded his school in the Lyceum at Athens, and presided over it for twelve years. Accused of irreligion by the anti-Macedonian party, he retired to Chalcis, where he died. Aristotle's philosophy shows traces of the profound influence of Plato upon him, but his method is wholly different, and he himself seems more conscious of divergence from his master than of agreement. In no department is the difference of his spirit and standpoint more striking than in that of Ethics.

The belief that the problem of practical life may be solved, if we can determine the nature of a supremely good and finally desirable end or goal of all action, and regard every part of our conduct as consisting in means to this end, which is the standard of all human life, has been the leading idea in a great deal of the history of thought about morals. The point of view is suggested in much that Plato writes, but it was first definitely and systematically stated as the central truth of Ethics, the one way to a rational existence, by Aristotle, in an unforgettably distinctive form.

The Doctrine of a Final End

THE NICOMACHEAN ETHICS I. i. Bywater's text has been used, as well as Grant's Edition of *The Nicomachean Ethics*.

Every art, and every pursuit, and enquiry, as likewise every act and purpose, seems to aim at some good. Therefore it has been well said that the good is that at which all things aim. But there appears to be a difference amongst ends. For sometimes the end consists in the exercise of a faculty for its own sake; at other times in certain external results beyond the activities. Now where there are ends beyond, in the case of these activities, the ends are regarded as higher than the activities. And since there are many actions and arts and sciences, many also are the ends that arise. For the end of medicine is health; the end of shipbuilding, a vessel;

142

of the military art, victory; of the industrial, wealth. Now where any of such activities are subordinate to some one art, even as the making of bridles is subordinate to horsemanship, as also are all the other instruments of the art of riding, whilst this and every warlike operation is subordinate to the military art, and in like manner other activities to other arts, in all such cases the ends of the master-art are more desirable than those which are instrumental to them. For it is for the sake of the former that the latter are pursued. And it makes no difference to this principle whether the development of the faculties or something else beyond these be the end of the actions, as in the examples of the sciences of which we have spoken.

ii.

If, then, there is some end of the practical activities which we desire for itself, desiring other things for the sake of this— and if we do not choose all that we choose with a view to something beyond, a pursuit which in its nature would go on to infinity, so that desire would be empty and vain— it is evident that this end would be the good and the best. And surely the knowledge of it would have great importance for life, and even as archers having a seen object to shoot at, we should the better hit the mark in our aim. Therefore, if this is so, the attempt must be made to sketch what it is in outline, and to which of the sciences or faculties it belongs. It would seem that it must belong to the most noble of these, the master-science.

Ethics and Politics

THE NICOMACHEAN ETHICS I. ii. It appeared to the Greek thinker to be in accordance with reason that there must be some supreme authority to lay down for the community the practical ideal, and therefore the duty of the citizen, morally as well as politically. These two aspects, indeed, were not so sharply differentiated by

Plato and Aristotle as in modern thought. And Aristotle believed in the State as capable of bringing out the highest potentialities of man in society.

This supreme art appears to be the political. For it is this which determines which of the sciences ought to have a place in cities, what kind of science each citizen should learn, and to what extent. We see also that the arts held most in honour are subordinate to this, such as the military art, the economic, and rhetoric, and that the rest of the practical arts make use of this. Moreover, we perceive that it issues regulations as to what acts ought to be done, and from which we ought to be restrained. The end of this art would then include the ends of all the others, so that in this would lie the good for man. For if the end is the same for the individual and the state, greater and more perfect would it be as the end for the state, both to attain and to preserve. Desirable indeed it is for one alone, but nobler and diviner for a race and states. The present study, then, is directed to this subject, being a kind of politics.

iv.

Since, then, every kind of knowledge and purpose aims at some good, what is that which we affirm to be the aim of the political art, and what the highest of all practical goods? In regard to its name there is agreement among the majority. For the multitude and the cultured alike call it well-being, and by this well-being they understand the same thing as living well and doing well. Yet concerning the nature of the soul's well-being they diverge in their views, and the many do not give the same account as the wise.

.   .   .   .   .   .

Determination of the Good for Man

THE NICOMACHEAN ETHICS I. vii.

Of what nature, then, is the good that we seek?

Since there appear to be many ends, and of these we choose

some for the sake of others, as for instance wealth, flutes and in general those that are instrumental, it is evident that not all these are final. But the best must be something final. If therefore there is only one final end, this would be what is sought, but, if more, the most final of these. Now we describe as more final that which is pursued for itself than that pursued for the sake of something else, and that which is never chosen on account of another end than the ends sought both for themselves and for the sake of something else, and absolutely final that which is always chosen for itself and never for anything beyond. And it is the soul's well-being which is in the highest sense this kind of end. For this we prefer always on its own account, and never for the sake of something else. It is otherwise with honour, and pleasure and intelligence and every excellence. We choose these, indeed, also for themselves, for though no further advantage were to accrue, we should choose to have them. Yet we choose them also for the sake of the soul's well-being, in the expectation that we shall find this well-being by these means. But no one chooses the soul's well-being for the sake of these, nor, speaking generally, on account of anything else. The same conclusion is seen to result also from consideration of self-sufficiency. For the perfect good seems to be something self-sufficient. By self-sufficiency we do not mean as for the individual alone, leading a solitary life, but for him as with parents and children and wife, and, in general, friends and fellow-citizens, since man is by nature social. What is self-sufficient we may again describe as that which, stripped of everything else, makes life desirable, and in lack of nothing. And such we think the soul's well-being to be. Happiness as the soul's well-being is then perfect and self-sufficient, being the end of all practical energies.

Well-being as the Fulfilment of the Essential Function of the Soul

In defining the best, however, as the well-being of the soul, we may seem to state the obvious, and it is desirable to explain more clearly what it is. Perhaps this would be best done by taking as our basis the function of man. For just as in the case of the flute-player and sculptor, and every artist, and in general for all who have some vocation and activity, their good and their well-being seems to lie in their function, so would it seem in the case of man as such. Are we indeed to suppose that there are functions and activities of the artisan and the shoemaker but not of man as man, and that he is constituted to be idle, with no special work of his own? Or even as there appears to be a special function of eye, and hand and foot, and generally of each of his members, so for man himself shall we lay down some function beyond all these? What then would this be?

Life indeed seems to be shared in common with plants, and it is the function that is special to man that we seek. The life of nutrition and growth must then be set aside. Next in order there is a life of sensation, but this also seems common to horse and ox and all animals. There remains a kind of practical life of a being possessed of reason. Now a part of the rational activity is, as it were, obedient to reason; the other element is that which reasons and understands. Seeing again that this may be thought of in two ways, we must lay down that it is the reason energising. For thus it is spoken of in its more essential aspect. The human good is then seen to be an energy of the soul in accordance with excellence, and if excellences be more than one, in accordance with the best and most perfect. Let us add—in a complete life, for one swallow does not make a spring, nor does a single day.

So is it that neither a single day, nor a short time, gives a man blessedness and inner well-being.

. . . . . .

(With this first sketch of the best life it is interesting and important to compare a further and somewhat different—indeed in certain respects strikingly different—conception of it, which is put before us by Aristotle in the last book of the *Ethics* from another standpoint. No longer the systematic teacher of the artistry of life, as it can be wrought into form by the average and practical citizen, he listens to and obeys a voice constraining him to speak of his own inmost experience. The well-being of the soul is after all only known for what it is by the individual soul, and the highest energy of the mind is a different energy for different minds. But perhaps Aristotle did not himself recognise all the implications of his dual account of the most perfect life.)

The Good for Man as Speculative

THE NICOMACHEAN ETHICS X. vi.

Having concluded the discussion of the virtues, and friendship and the pleasures, it remains to consider the subject of the soul's well-being, since we assigned this as the end and summit of human things. We said that it is not a habit, for in that case it might belong to one who slept through life, living a vegetable existence, and to one who was unfortunate in the greatest matters. But if this idea must be rejected, and it ought rather to be conceived as a certain energy, as was earlier said, whilst amongst energies some are necessary and chosen for the sake of others, and some are chosen for themselves, it is evident that well-being must be placed amongst those which are chosen for themselves.

(Aristotle refers to the conclusion that well-being is an end desired for itself alone, and distinguishes this desire from those for objects pursued as children pursue their pleasures, and proceeds)—

6.

We choose all things, so to speak, for the sake of something else except well-being. For this is the end. And to labour and toil for the sake of amusement would seem foolish and too childish. But to indulge in play so that one may be earnest in work, as Anaxagoras says, seems to be the right way. For

amusement is a relaxation. Unable ceaselessly to labour we need
a pause. But the relaxation is not the end, for it is for the
sake of the energy. And the life of well-being is in accordance
with excellence, and this with seriousness, and not with play.
vii.

If, then, the well-being of the soul is an energy in accordance with excellence, it is reasonable that it should be in
accordance with the highest excellence, and this would be
the excellence of the noblest part. Now whether this is mind,
or whatever else it be, which seems to govern and lead by
nature, and to have insight, in regard to what is noble and
divine, whether as being itself divine, or the most divine of
the faculties within us, it is the activity of this in accordance
with its own excellence which is the perfect well-being of
life. That this is a theoretic activity, has been said. And this
would seem to be in accord both with what has preceded
and with the truth. For this is the mightiest energy—since
mind is the greatest of the elements in ourselves, and of
objects of knowledge those are the greatest to which mind
is directed. Moreover this is the most uninterrupted activity.
For we are able to exercise the speculative vision con-
tinuously more than any other activity. We believe again
that pleasure must be mingled with this well-being, for the
energy which belongs to wisdom is agreed to be the sweetest.

Philosophy then appears to possess pleasures the most
wonderful in purity and stability, and it is reasonable to
suppose that the possession of truth is a sweeter experience
than the search for it. And what we call self-sufficiency would
attend most on the theoretic activity. For as concerns the
things necessary for life, men require them in so far as they
are wise and just, and in all other capacities. And once he is
sufficiently provided with such things, the just man must
have people in relation to and with whom he will perform
just acts, and equally so the temperate, and the courageous,

and the rest. But the wise man can speculate in solitude, and the more so in proportion to his wisdom. Better is it for him perhaps if he have fellow-workers, but nevertheless he is the most self-sufficient. And it would seem that this activity alone is loved for itself. For nothing results from it beyond the exercise of reason, whereas in the case of practical activities we gain something whether more or less as a result of the action. And the soul's well-being seems to be found in leisure. For we sacrifice leisure for the sake of enjoying leisure, and we wage war in order to be at peace.

Now the exercise of the practical excellences is in the political or the military life, and activities in these spheres seem to be without rest, especially those of war. But the political function is also devoid of leisure, and beyond the business of politics it aims at offices and honours. Or if it aims at well-being itself, for the individual and his fellow-citizens, it aims at this as something lying beyond the political life, since we seek it in addition to this. Seeing then that amongst pursuits which have most prestige, the political and the military excel in nobility and greatness, and notwithstanding are laborious and directed to some end, and not chosen on their own account, whilst the energy of the mind as speculative seems to surpass in value and to aim at no end beyond itself, and to possess its own peculiar pleasure (which in turn stimulates the energy); and if the experiences attendant on this energy are self-sufficient and free and inexhaustible, so far as anything human can be so, and have whatever else characterises blessedness, this would be the perfect well-being of the soul, assuming a complete term of life. For there is nothing imperfect in the conditions of well-being. A life of this kind would be greater than that of man, for it is not possible thus to live in so far as human, but in so far as something divine is present in us. In proportion as this surpasses the life of the composite being, by so much does the energy of this life excel that of other excellences. And if reason is divine in relation to man, so also the life of this kind is divine in comparison with human life. But we must not follow those who counsel us, being men, to think the thoughts of man, and being mortal, mortal things, but in so far as possible we should be immortal, and do everything in order to live in accordance with the highest within us.

For though it be small in bulk, in power and dignity it far exceeds all the rest. Moreover it would seem that it is in this that each of us finds his truest being, if it is the nobler and better. And strange indeed would it be if one were to choose not one's own life but that of some other. What was said earlier accords with the present discourse. For whatever is most native to the constitution of anything in nature is best and most pleasant for it. And of a certainty the life of reason is thus for man, if it is this which is above all the man himself. It is he therefore who has also the highest well-being of the soul.

vii.
(Many things are needed for action, and in general the greater and nobler the action, the more scenery it requires.)
6.
But to the seeker after truth there is need of none of these things in addition to his scientific activity, but they will even be a hindrance to speculation. As man and living among men he will choose the conduct which accords with virtue. He will therefore have need of such things in order to the human life. But that the perfect well-being of the soul lies in the theoretic energy, is evident also from the following consideration, namely, we conceive the Gods as having blessedness in the supreme sense, and well-being.

Life of the Gods
But what kind of practical activities is it fitting to ascribe to them? Those of just dealing forsooth? Or would it not

seem ridiculous to suppose that they have commercial transactions, and exchange deposits and do similar business? Or those of courage?—enduring terrible things, and risking themselves because it is noble? Or perchance those of liberality? But to whom shall they give? Out of place surely amongst them would be money and the like. What would be their acts of temperance? Nay, unseemly would be the praise that they have no low desires. Should we go through the whole list, it would appear that all affairs of practice are small and unworthy of the Gods. Nevertheless, all men conceive them as living and energising; not indeed slumbering as Endymion. Now when we conceive a living being without action and *a fortiori* all doing of deeds, what remains except speculative thought? Hence the energy of God, surpassing in blessedness, would be the theoretic. And amongst human activities that which is most akin to this is the truest well-being of the soul. A sign of this is that the other animals do not share in happiness as the soul's well-being, wholly lacking as they do this kind of energy. For the Gods the whole of life is blessed; for men it is so in so far as a reflection of this energy is experienced. Of the other animals none knows the soul's well-being, since they never share in speculation. So far as speculation can extend, so far well-being; and for those to whom speculation is more possible, so also well-being, not as something accidental but through its very nature. For this energy is in itself sublime. It follows that the soul's well-being consists in a kind of contemplation.

The Virtues or Excellences

It is Aristotle's treatment of virtue which illuminates for us best the conception of a satisfactory or valuable life which belongs to Greek intellectualism.

Plato is always thinking of the extraordinary, the grand types of life, by means of which reform may come, the uncompromising upholder of the very truth, the mind which, having the vision of the eternal good, attempts to realise this very vision in its colourless

N

beauty in the actual world. Aristotle's virtuous or excellent citizen can find a sphere in which he fully expands in all his powers, the civic environment which he was not born only to set right. What are his chief excellences?

(In Aristotle's first account of the elements of the soul, as we have seen, he distinguishes three aspects. In a later passage he suggests that we may attribute a kind of secondary rationality to the appetitive or desiring part of the soul, in so far as it is directed by reason. This determines the distinction of two kinds of virtue or excellence, moral and intellectual.)

THE NICOMACHEAN ETHICS I. xiii.

It may be said (from one point of view) that the rational part of the soul is dual, the one element possessing reason essentially and as ruling; the other being rational in so far as it renders obedience as to a father. Now the virtues may be classified in accordance with this distinction. For we speak of certain virtues as intellectual, certain as moral; for example, wisdom and understanding and practical thought are intellectual, liberality and temperance, moral. When we are discussing matters of morals we do not say that a man is wise or keen-witted, but that he is gentle or temperate.

Virtue neither Innate, nor Contrary to Nature

THE NICOMACHEAN ETHICS II. i.

Excellence is then of two kinds, the one intellectual, the other moral. Now intellectual excellence has for the most part both its origin and its growth in teaching, and on this account is in need of experience and time. Moral virtue on the other hand develops from habit, whence also it has acquired the name ethical, with a slight deflection from Ethos (custom). Hence it is evident that none of the moral virtues comes to us by nature. For none of the things that are by nature can be trained in another direction. The stone, for instance, by nature tending downwards, could not be trained to tend upwards, not if one should accustom it by throwing it upwards ten thousand times. Neither could fire acquire the habit of going downwards, nor could any of those things which by nature behave in one way be trained to behave otherwise. Neither then by nature, nor against nature, do the virtues arise, but we are fitted to acquire them and are perfected in them through habit. Moreover in regard to our natural capacities, we are endowed with the faculties, which we later exhibit in operation—as for instance in the case of sight. . . . But we acquire the virtuous capacities through practising ourselves in the acts, as is the case also with the arts. For it is by doing that we learn those acts, which having learned we ought to do, as for instance, by building we become builders, and by flute-playing, flute-players. Thus also, by doing just acts we become just; by temperate acts, temperate; by courageous acts, courageous. In one word, states of mind are developed out of the activities which correspond to them. Therefore we ought to perform the appropriate energies, for different characters will result from different actions. It makes no small difference, then, whether our training from youth upwards is of this kind or that. Rather it makes a very great difference, if not the whole

The Doctrine of the Mean

THE NICOMACHEAN ETHICS II. ii. Having emphasised the practical nature of the study, Aristotle observes that one principle to bear in mind is that the practical qualities we are examining are liable to be injured or destroyed both by defect and excess. This is the case also with strength and health. So are temperance, courage. and the other virtues destroyed by defect and excess and preserved through moderation. The genus or general nature of virtue as a habit of mind, or formed state of the dispositions, is determined. But we have to consider what Aristotle speaks of in logical terminology as the differentia. What kind of habit or settled disposition?

THE NICOMACHEAN ETHICS II. vi. The hint thrown out about the fatal effects alike of excess and defect, further developed, gives the answer.

In all quantity, both continuous and discrete, we can have a more, a less, and an equal, either from the point of view of the object, or in relation to ourselves. Now the equal is a mean between excess and defect. . . . When I speak of the mean in relation to the object, I signify that which is equally distant from both extremes—this is one and the same for all. The mean relatively to us is, on the other hand, that which is neither excessive nor defective, and this is not one and the same for all. For example, if ten be too many and two too few, we assume six to be the mean in an absolute sense, since it is greater and less by the same amount. And this is the mean according to arithmetical proportion. But the mean relatively to ourselves is not to be conceived in this way. Every man of understanding avoids both excess and deficiency, and seeks and chooses the mean; not however the absolute, but the relative mean. Every art thus completes its work by observing the mean, and conducting its results to this. On this account we are accustomed to say of works well-performed that there is nothing to be added to or taken away from them, implying that anything more or less than this would destroy its perfection, and the mean conserve it.

Since then, as we say, good artists do their work with this in view, virtue like nature being more accurate and superior to every art, would be that which aims at the mean. I speak, of course, of the ethical mean. For this is concerned with emotions and actions, and it is in these that there is both excess and defect, and the mean. Thus it is possible to fear and rejoice, and desire, and be angry, to feel pity, and in general to feel pleasure and pain both more or less, and in either case not well. But to have these feelings at the right time, and on occasion of the right things, and towards the right persons, and with the right object, and in the right manner, this is the golden mean, and the highest excellence, names which are proper to virtue. And so it is with actions, there is excess and defect, and the mean. Now virtue has to do with emotions and actions, spheres in which both excess and defect is error, whilst the mean is praised and is right— indications these of excellence. A kind of moderation therefore is virtue, since it aims at the mean. Moreover, error is of many forms, for evil is of the nature of the infinite, as the Pythagoreans represented, and good of the finite. There is only one way of doing right. Therefore the former is easy, the latter difficult. For it is easy to miss the mark; difficult to hit it. And on this account there is excess and defect in evil and the mean in virtue.

Excellent things are simple in nature; evil, variegated.

Virtue, then, is a purposeful habit, lying in the mean relatively to us, defined by reason and as the wise man would define it. It is the mean between two evils, the one of excess, the other of defect. Therefore viewed in the light of its essence and conception for definition, virtue is a mean, but from the point of view of supreme excellence and rightness it is an extreme.

ILLUSTRATIONS OF ARISTOTLE'S TREATMENT OF THE SPECIAL VIRTUES

The reader of Aristotle's *Ethics* may be surprised at the wide range of the aspects of character and action treated as moral virtues, in addition to the four leading virtues of Plato's *Republic* and other dialogues. We have to remember that the Greek word for virtue should often, especially in Aristotle's use of it, be translated as excellence, and that the "excellences" of Aristotle's *Ethics* are intended to bring before us the bearing of the cultured citizen in all the ordinary experiences of social life. Some of them imply the possession of a great position and great resources, and their inclusion helps us to interpret Aristotle's view that certain external advantages are necessary to the best life. He gives us his conception, not merely of the highest fulfilment of duty, but of the highest value which can be got out of life, in the most favourable circumstances. The latter, indeed, is the leading aspect and significance of the study of the high-souled man who is the hero of Aristotle's *Ethics*. The passages which follow show the distinctive Aristotelian treatment of the cardinal virtue of courage, a sublimation of the Homeric spirit, as perhaps we may call it, and the still more distinctive portrayal of the ideal citizen in the account of liberality and the character-sketch of the great-souled man.

Courage

THE NICOMACHEAN ETHICS III. v., vi.

First let us consider courage. That it is a mean or moderation, in relation to fear and confidence, has been said. And it is obvious that we fear what is fearful; that is, to speak generally, what is evil. Fear has therefore been defined— expectation of evil. Now we dread all evils, such as disgrace, poverty, disease, friendlessness, death. But the courage of the brave man does not seem to be called forth by all these things. For some of them ought to be dreaded, and it is noble to dread them, as, for instance, disgrace, and not to dread them is shameful. In such cases he who fears is righteous and modest; he who fears not, shameless. But by some this kind of fearless person is called courageous, metaphorically. For he has some resemblance to the man of courage, since he also is without fear. And perhaps one ought not to fear poverty nor disease, nor in general those things that are not the result of vice, nor of one's own action. Still it is not the man who is fearless in these matters whom we call courageous.

.   .   .   .   .   .

In relation, then, to what kind of terrors is a man courageous? Surely those that are greatest. For there is no one better able than he to stand fast before what is terrible. And most terrible is death. For it is the end, and nothing more seems to be left for the dead, whether good or evil. However, it seems that not even in regard to death universally is a man judged courageous; as, for instance, death at sea, or from illness. In what forms of death then? Surely in the noblest. Such are those of war. For death in war is met in the greatest and noblest danger.

This estimate is in harmony with the bestowal of honours in cities and in kingdoms. In the essential sense, then, he would be called courageous who is without fear in the presence of a noble death, and in regard to things which suddenly bring on death. Not but that the man of courage is fearless when at sea, or in illness; but his fearlessness will be of a different kind from that of the sailors. For the former gives up all hope of rescue, whilst the sailors are of good cheer because of experience. Moreover, the courageous show their valour where there is aid to render, and glory in dying, and neither is present in the type of danger just referred to.

.   .   .   .   .   .

ix.

Though courage is concerned both with occasions of confidence and of fear, it is not equally concerned with both, but more with the fearful. For it is he who is unperturbed, and bears himself as he ought in these crises, rather than in those that awaken confidence, who is courageous. And as has been said, men are called courageous for endurance of what is painful. Therefore does courage bring him pain, and justly is it praised. For harder is it to endure pain than to renounce pleasure. Not but that the end which belongs to courage seems pleasant, but this pleasantness is apt to be concealed by the attendant circumstances as happens in the athletic contests. For to the boxers the end at which they aim is sweet, the crown and honours, but the blows, and indeed the whole labour, are painful and grievous to flesh to endure. And because these painful conditions are many, and small the prize for which they suffer, there seems to be no pleasure. If, then, it is thus with courage, death and wounds are indeed painful to the brave man and undesired by him, but he endures these things because it is noble, or because not to endure is base. And in proportion to his possession of all excellence and of the soul's good, by so much the more will he be grieved at death. For to such a man life is most worth living, and he is deprived of the things of greatest value, knowing their worth. And this is a painful thing. None the less is he valiant; perhaps, indeed, all the more, for he chooses what is noble in war rather than these things. Nor does pleasure attend on the exercise of all the virtues, except in so far as their end is attained.

Liberality

THE NICOMACHEAN ETHICS IV. i. 12. Liberality has been defined as the mean or right kind of action in the sphere of property, concerning the giving and receiving of money, but especially the giving and spending. Prodigality and illiberality are the extremes and deficiencies in the same sphere.

The liberal man will give for the sake of what is noble, and in the right way. For he makes his gift to whom he ought, and the right amount, at the right time, and in all respects in accordance with the right spirit of giving. And this he does with pleasure, or without pain; certainly not with pain. But he who gives where he should not give, or not for a noble motive, but for some other cause, must not be described as liberal but in some other way. Nor he who gives grudgingly. For this man would prefer his goods to a noble deed, and this is not the spirit of a liberal man. Nor will the liberal man accept from any quarter where he ought not. For such an acceptance is not the sort of thing to be done by one who does not value wealth. Nor would he be ready to ask favours. For to accept benefits gladly is not the way of the benefactor.

He will not be neglectful of his resources, since he desires to provide for others from these. Nor will he give indiscriminately, so that he may have the wherewithal to give to the right persons, at the right time and nobly. And it belongs to the liberal man to be zealous and to exceed in

giving, so that he leaves less for himself. Liberality is esti-
mated in relation to means. For it does not consist in the
amount of what is given, but in the habit of giving, and
this is in accordance with the means. There is no reason why
the greater liberality should not lie in the smaller gift, if
made out of smaller resources. More liberal seem those who
have not acquired but have inherited their possessions. For
they are inexperienced in want, and all are apt to love more
their own productions, as do parents and poets. It is not
easy for the generous man to be rich, since he neither takes
nor guards what he has but is lavish, and does not value
money for itself but for the sake of gifts. Therefore fate is
blamed because those who are most worthy are least wealthy.
But it is not unreasonable that this should be so; for it is not
possible to have possessions, if one takes no trouble about it
any more than in any other matter.

26.

The liberal man is easy to deal with in matters of money.
Indeed he is liable to be cheated, since he sets no store by it.
And he is more vexed if he has neglected any fitting
occasion of spending, than pained if he has spent where it
was not needed. But the extravagant man goes wrong also
in these respects.

It has been said that extravagance and illiberality are the
forms of excess and defect shown both in giving and in
taking, for expenditure is included in what is given away.
Now extravagance goes to excess, both in giving and in not
receiving, and shows its defect in taking. The defect of
illiberality is in giving, and its excess in grasping, only it is
in petty matters that it is exhibited. The two sides of extravagance do not often exist together. For it is not easy for

those who receive nothing to give to all. The resources of private persons (and only these can be regarded as extravagant) soon fail. The prodigal may be held not a little better than the illiberal. For he is easily cured both by increasing years and by lack of means, and can be brought to the *juste milieu*. He has indeed the qualities of the liberal man, since he gives and does not take, though he does neither in the right or best way. If, then, he be educated in this respect, or for some other cause should change, he would be liberal. For he would then both give where he ought and not take where he ought not. And so the character does not seem to be a poor one, for it does not belong to a bad, nor to an ignoble man, to give away lavishly, without taking in return, but rather to a simpleton. A prodigal of this kind, then, seems to be much better than an illiberal man, both on account of the causes we have mentioned, and because he is helpful to many, while the illiberal does not help anyone, not even himself. Most prodigals, however, as we have implied, also grasp where they should not, and are in this respect illiberal.

For they become grasping through the desire to spend, not finding it easy to do this, since their resources are quickly exhausted, and they are forced to obtain more elsewhere. Moreover, because they have no high ideal, they spend recklessly on all occasions. For they want to give, and the question how or whence makes no difference. Hence their gifts are not nobly given with a noble aim, nor in the right way. Thus, sometimes they enrich those who should be poor, giving nothing to those whose characters are modest, but much to flatterers or those who procure for them some other pleasure. And so the majority of them are profligate —for they spend readily and are lavish in expenditure on self-indulgence. And through failure to live for the moral ideal, they incline to pleasures. Thus the prodigal man, if not disciplined by education, follows this sort of rake's progress. If, however, he chance on guidance, he may arrive at the golden mean and the strait way. But illiberality is incurable, for age and every kind of infirmity seem to make people illiberal, and this vice is more engrained in human nature than prodigality, and the majority are rather lovers of money than spendthrift.

.   .   .   .   .   .

The High-souled or Lofty-spirited Man

THE NICOMACHEAN ETHICS IV. iii.

The man of lofty spirit is worthy of great things, and he knows this. For the man who does not make claims in accordance with his worth is foolish, and in excellence there is no folly or stupidity. . . . Now the man of little worth who knows himself for what he is, has a modest disposition, but not a high soul. For loftiness of spirit implies greatness, as beauty needs a large frame. The small may be graceful and well-proportioned but not beautiful. He who thinks himself great when unworthy of it is vain, though not everyone who thinks of himself more highly than he ought to think is vain. He who thinks of himself less than he ought to think has a petty soul, whatever his true worth, whether great or moderate, or little, he thinks too little of it. Now the high-souled man is at the highest point in respect to greatness, but he observes the mean in so far as he thinks of himself as he ought to think. He esteems himself in accordance with his worth, whilst others think either too highly or too meanly of themselves. . . . Now value has relation to external goods. And we regard as greatest that good which we render to the Gods, and to which those most aspire who are held in esteem, and which is the prize in the noblest contests. Now this is honour, for it is the greatest of external goods. It is then in the sphere of honour and dishonour that the high-souled man is what he ought to be. Without argument, indeed, it is evident that high-minded men are concerned with honour. For they claim honour most of all, and claim it worthily. . . . The high-souled man since he is worthy of the greatest things is the best. For he who is better is worthy of the greater, and he who is best of the greatest. He who is truly high-minded must then be good. And greatness in every form of excellence would seem characteristic of the high-souled man. In no wise would it befit him to take to his heels with limbs quaking, nor to be unjust. For why should he to whom nothing is of great moment act unjustly? Whatever aspect of the matter we consider, it would seem ridiculous to conceive the great-souled man to be lacking in goodness. For if without character, he would not be worthy of honour, since the reward of virtue is honour, and it is rendered to the good. Loftiness of spirit appears then to be the crown of the virtues, for it both enhances them and presupposes them. Hence it is difficult to have this loftiness in very truth, for it is not possible without moral beauty. Above all, the great-souled character is shown in the realm of honour and dishonour. And where great honours from noble sources are concerned, he feels but a moderate delight, as one who receives his due, or even less than his due. For there is no honour worthy of perfect virtue. Not but that he will accept it, inasmuch as the world has nothing greater to offer him. But he will make little of what is offered him by inconsiderable persons on slight grounds, since he is worthy of greater things. As regards dishonour, it could not rightly come nigh him. Although, as we have said, honour is especially the field of the great-souled man, he will not less observe due moderation in regard to riches and the exercise of rule, and in every kind of fortune, good and ill, whatever befall, neither overjoyed at prosperity nor downcast at adversity.

For he is not moved in these ways, even in the matter of honour, the greatest thing of all. And it is for the sake of honour that power and wealth are desirable. For those who possess these things hope for honour on their account. Now to the man for whom honour is a small matter, other things are also small. Hence there is a touch of scorn in men of lofty spirit. It is generally supposed that good fortune contributes to high-mindedness. For the well-born—the ruling and the wealthy classes—are treated with honour, since they are in a superior position, and to have the superiority in any good thing is more honourable. Thus things of this kind minister to loftiness of spirit, since there are some who accord honour to them. In truth, however, the good alone ought to be honoured, though to him who has both more honour accrues. Those who possess these other goods are mistaken in thinking themselves worthy of greatness, if they lack virtue, nor is it right to term them high-minded. For without virtue it is not easy to bear good fortune with grace. Unable to endure prosperity and supposing themselves to excel over others, they despise these, and in their own actions do as chance suggests. As they imitate the high-souled man without being like him, they imitate where they can. His excellences they cannot rival, but they show contempt to others. Now the man of lofty spirit despises justly (for his estimate is true), but most people show contempt at random.

He is not a man to expose himself to danger for trifles, nor is he a lover of danger, because his reverence is given to few things, but he is ready to meet great dangers, and whenever he risks himself, he is unsparing of his life, as something not worth saving at all costs. He is one to confer benefits, and to shrink from receiving them, for the one befits a superior, the other an inferior. And he will repay the service with a greater. Thus he who began the kindness will more abundantly receive and be the gainer. These men, moreover, seem to have better memories for the benefits they have conferred than for those conferred on them, for the recipient of a benefit is in an inferior position to the benefactor, and superiority is what they desire. References to the first they hear with pleasure, but to the second with pain.

It belongs also to the high-souled man to be in need of nothing or hardly anything, and to be zealous in the service he renders, and to bear himself loftily towards persons of estimation and prosperity, but with urbanity to those of modest fortunes. For to overtop the former is a difficult and distinguished thing; in the other case it is easy. And to be of a lofty demeanour is not ill-bred in such company; but amongst the humbler sort it would show a lack of good manners, like a display of strength amongst the weak. Neither will he be occupied with things commonly esteemed, or those in which others excel. And he will be leisurely and unhurried, except where some great honour or action calls him, and busied about only a few matters, but those great and renowned. He is of necessity an open enemy and open friend, for concealment belongs to timidity, and he regards truth rather than appearance. He is open both in word and deed, free of speech, because lofty in thought, and truthful, except where irony is in place. He is ironic towards the multitude. And he is incapable of accommodating his life to that of another, unless it be a friend; for that would be servile. Hence all flatterers are menial, and the lowly are flatterers. The great-souled man is not easily moved to admiration, for nothing is great in his eyes. Nor is he mindful of wrong; for it is not magnanimous to be over-mindful, especially of wrong, but rather to overlook. Nor is his conversation about persons, for he speaks neither of himself nor of another. He is not anxious about praise for himself or blame for others. Nor is he given to praising, nor for the same reason to evil-speaking, not even of his enemies, unless from contempt. And about necessaries or petty matters, he is least liable to complain, or entreat, as accords with the bearing of a man of weight. His possessions are rather what is beautiful and brings no profit, than things profitable and useful, a characteristic of independence. His movement is slow, his voice deep, his manner of speech tranquil. For the man who gives his serious interest only to a few things is not in a hurry nor overstrained, since nothing seems great to him. And haste and a high-pitched voice are produced by that illusion.

Such is the man of lofty spirit; one who is deficient in this respect is little-minded; he who exceeds arrogant. . . . The small-minded man though deserving of good things deprives himself of those things of which he is worthy, and seems to have some defect through not appreciating his own claims, and through ignorance of himself, else he would have aimed at the good things he had a claim to.

.   .   .   .   .   .

As for the boastful, they are foolish and self-ignorant, and that most obviously, for they aim at honours, as though they were worthy, and are proved incapable.

.   .   .   .   .   .

Yet little-mindedness is more antithetic to the great-souled type than is self-exaltation. For it is more common and meaner.

On the Voluntary and the Involuntary

THE NICOMACHEAN ETHICS III. i. Aristotle's consideration of this subject covers what he has to say on the subject which we should discuss as the will. It has been noticed that this problem has not quite the same significance for the Greek as for the modern moralist. Yet Aristotle's treatment is an excellent introduction to the history of European thought on this theme.

Since virtue depends upon feelings and actions, and praise and blame are occasioned when action is voluntary, whilst there is sympathy or at times compassion when it is involuntary, it is surely necessary in an investigation of virtue, to define the voluntary and involuntary as also useful for those who legislate in regard to rewards and punishments. It seems that involuntary actions are those done under compulsion or through ignorance. And by actions done under compulsion we mean those of which the origin is external, of the kind to which he who acts or suffers contributes nothing, as for instance when a wind carries you in any direction or men in whose power you are. There is a difficulty in connection with acts which are done through fear of greater evils, or for some noble object, whether they are voluntary or involuntary, as, for example, if a tyrant have a man's wife and children in his power and performance of the act would save them, failure to perform cause their death. Something of this kind happens in the case of throwing cargo overboard in storms. For no one would cast it away willingly, but to save himself and others, everyone capable of reflection would do it. Actions of this kind, then, seem to be mixed in character, but to resemble more the voluntary. For they are choice-worthy at the time when they are done, and the moral character of the action is determined by the circumstances; and the terms voluntary and involuntary are ascribed to the act at the moment of doing it. Now in such cases it is done voluntarily. For the cause of the movement of the organic members in actions of this kind is in the person himself. And where the cause is in oneself, it lies in oneself both to do and to forbear. Such acts, then, are voluntary, though in the abstract perhaps involuntary, for no one would choose on its own account any action of this kind. For actions like this, people are sometimes praised, when they endure something shameful or painful for the sake of what is great and noble. But if otherwise, they are blamed. For to suffer what is shameful for an object either not noble or only moderately so, shows a mean nature. In certain cases, though there is no praise there is pity; that is when a man does what he ought not to do for considerations which it exceeds human nature to resist, and no one could withstand. But in some cases, perhaps, it is not meet to yield to such compulsion, and one ought rather to die, suffering even what is most terrible. The grounds, for instance, compelling the Alcmæon of Euripides to slay his mother seem ridiculous. And it is sometimes difficult to decide which kind of contingency ought to be preferred, and of two dire alternatives which should be endured, and yet more difficult to abide by our conclusion.

Now what kind of actions should be called compulsory? Shall we say in general that the action is compulsory whenever the cause lies in what is external and the agent contributes nothing to the event? As regards the actions which are in themselves involuntary, but at the moment and as compared with other alternatives desirable, and of which the principle is in the agent, these, though in their own nature involuntary, are now relatively to others voluntary. They are, however, more of the voluntary type. For actions lie in particulars, and as particular they are voluntary. . . . But if anyone were to say that what is done with a view to pleasant or to noble ends is necessitated (for these motives exercise compulsion and are external), his argument would prove all action to be compulsory, for all action whatever is for the sake of these objects. And those who act from compulsion and unwillingly do it with pain, those who are induced by the motives of pleasant and noble ends, with pleasure. It is absurd to blame external conditions and not oneself as too easily ensnared by things of this kind, and to attribute to oneself the noble deeds, to the lure of pleasure the base. That action, then, is compulsory, of which the source is external, the person under compulsion not contributing anything to it.

o

Now that which is done through ignorance is always non-voluntary, but it is involuntary only when it causes pain and remorse. For he who does anything in ignorance, if in no way distressed at the deed, did not indeed act voluntarily, since he did not know, but neither involuntarily seeing that, he did not feel pain. He, then, who repents of what he did in ignorance seems to have been unwilling; he who is unrepentant, since he differs from the former, shall be called a non-voluntary agent. For since he is of a distinct type, it is better he should have a special name. There seems to be a further distinction between acting on account of ignorance, or in a state of ignorance. The man who is intoxicated or in a rage does not seem to act on account of ignorance, but in consequence of drunkenness or anger, yet not wittingly, but in a state of ignorance. For every depraved man is ignorant of what he ought to do, and from what he ought to refrain, and on account of this kind of error, men become unjust and in general bad. But the word involuntary should not be used of one who is ignorant of his true interest. For ignorance of principle is not the cause of involuntary action, but of vice. Neither is ignorance of the universal to be so regarded (since for this people are blamed), but of the particulars which are the circumstances and the objects of action. It is ignorance of these which calls for compassion and pardon. For he who is unaware of any of these details acts involuntarily.

.   .   .   .   .   .

Ignorance, then, being concerned with all the circumstances of the action, he that is ignorant of some one of these is held to have acted involuntarily, and especially if ignorant with regard to the most important, and the most important seem to be the objects of the action, and the tendency of it. The act of the person who can be described as involuntary in his deed on account of this kind of ignorance, must also be a cause of pain to him, and of repentance.

Since the involuntary has been shown to be that act which is done under compulsion, and because of ignorance, voluntary would appear to be that action of which the principle is in the doer himself, knowing the particular circumstances in which the act lies. For, perhaps it was not well said that acts done in passion or desire are involuntary. In the first place, if this were so, none of the other animals would act voluntarily, nor children. Secondly, are we to say that none of the acts caused by desire and passion are voluntary, or that our noble acts are voluntary, the base involuntary? Or is this absurd since there is one cause of both, and perhaps it is odd to call involuntary our desires for what ought to be desired? There are also things about which one ought to be angry, and things one ought to wish for, such as health and learning; and that which is involuntary is thought to be painful; that which accords with desire pleasant. Again, how do sins of reflection differ from sins of passion in respect to this character of involuntariness? For both should be avoided. And the irrational states seem to be not less human than the rational, and so, therefore, also the actions of man which proceed from passion and desire. It would indeed be strange to set these down as involuntary.

ii.

The voluntary and involuntary having been defined, the subject of purpose should be next considered; for it seems to be most intimately connected with virtue, and to be a better criterion of character than conduct. Purpose seems certainly to be voluntary, but is not the same thing, for the sphere of the voluntary is wider; for children and the other animals share in the capacity for voluntary action, but not in that of purpose, and we speak of suddenness in the case of voluntary actions, but not of purpose.

(Aristotle proceeds to distinguish purpose from desire, passion, opinion, wish. It is the man of self-control who is a man of purpose, and purpose is opposed to desire. It does not aim at pleasure or pain, like desire; nor at the impossible [as for instance to escape death], like wish.)

No one makes what is impracticable the object of his purpose, but what he thinks can be brought about by himself. Again, wish is directed rather to the end, purpose to the means to the end; we wish, for instance, for health; we purpose those things through which we become healthy. And we wish to have true happiness and say so, but it is not suitable to say that we purpose it. In general, it seems that purpose is directed to the things which are in our power. . . . It is voluntary, but not all that is voluntary is purposive. What distinguishes purpose is previous deliberation; for purpose is attended with reason and thought, the name seems to indicate this, signifying chosen before other courses.

The True Good or the Seeming as Object of Desire and Action

THE NICOMACHEAN ETHICS III. iv.

It has been said that the object of desire is the end; but some think that this is the good; others that it is the apparent good. This leads to the result that for those who say the good is the object of wish, what he wills who does not choose rightly is not willed (for if it was willed, it was good; and in this case it happened not to be good). For those, on the other hand, who say that the good is what seems good, it results that there is no object of desire which is such in the nature of things, but the object is as it seems to every individual. Now different, and as it may happen, contrary ends seem good to different people.

If these results are not satisfactory, must we not say that absolutely, and in truth, the good is the object of desire, but to every individual, the seeming good? Therefore to the good man it is the good in truth; to the unworthy any chance object. Similarly in the case of the body, for those that

are in a good condition, that is healthful which is really
so; but it is otherwise with those suffering from disease; and
in like manner with what is bitter and sweet, hot, heavy, and
other sensations. The good man has a right judgment in all
things, and in every case he perceives the truth. For every
special disposition what is noble and pleasant appears in
special form, and the good man is perhaps distinguished above
all by his ability to discern the truth in each case, being
as it were a standard and measure. Amongst the majority
delusion seems to arise through pleasure; for though not
the good, it seems to be good. Therefore they choose pleasure
as good and flee pain as evil.

Vice equally Voluntary with Virtue

The Nicomachean Ethics III. v.

Inasmuch, then, as the object of wish is the end, and
deliberation and purpose are concerned with the means to
the end, the actions that are concerned with the means
must be in accordance with purpose, and voluntary. The
energies of the virtues have to do with means. Virtue, then,
depends on ourselves, and equally so vice; for where it lies
in ourselves to do, so also not to do. And where it is for us
to say " no," so again to say " yes." It results that if performance when noble lies with us, so also failure to perform
when this is base. And if resistance to action when noble
is in our power, so also to yield to action when base. If it
depends on ourselves to do acts both noble and base, it does
so equally not to do them, and this means as we saw to become good or bad men. It is then in our own power to be
righteous or unworthy. Now the statement that no one is
voluntarily evil, or unwillingly blest, is partly false and partly
true. It is true that no one is blest against his will, yet vice
is voluntary. Or what has just been said must be contested,

and man not allowed to be a source of actions, nor their begetter as of children. But if this does seem so and we have no other principles to which to relate our actions beyond those in ourselves, those deeds of which the principles are in ourselves are themselves our own and voluntary. To this there seems to be witness both in every individual's private experience and in the public proceedings of the legislators themselves. For those who commit crimes, when acting neither under compulsion nor through ignorance for which they were not themselves responsible, are punished, and those who perform noble acts rewarded, as though to encourage these, and deter the others. And yet no one urges us to do what is not within our power, nor voluntary, inasmuch as exhortations are of no avail in such matters, as, for instance, not to grow heated, or suffer pain or hunger or anything of this kind; for none the less shall we suffer these things. Nay, ignorance itself is punished if a man seem to be the cause of his ignorance, as with drunkards, the penalties are double. This is because the beginning is in his power; for he had it in his own power not to be in this state, and it was this that caused his ignorance. Those also who are ignorant of any matters of law, which they ought to know, and which are not difficult, are punished, and similarly in other matters of which people seem to be ignorant through neglect, inasmuch as it is incumbent on them not to be ignorant; for it was in their power to take precautions against this. Perhaps it may be objected, He is the sort of person to be inattentive to these things. But these men are themselves responsible for being that kind of person through loose living, and for being unjust or intemperate, some through acting unrighteously, others through spending their time in drinking and the like. For it is practice in particular acts which makes people such as to do these acts. . . . Again, it is unreasonable to presume that the man who does unjust deeds does not want to be unjust, or the doer of intemperate acts not to be intemperate. If, then, without the excuse of ignorance, a man does those actions through which he will become unjust, he is willingly unjust, though not for mere willing can he cease from injustice and be just. Neither can the sick man become well by such means. It may even happen that he is willingly sick, because he lives incontinently and disobeys the physician. Once, indeed, it was possible for him not to be sick, but now that he has thrown his health away, it is so no longer, just as it is not possible for one who has thrown a stone away to recover it. Nevertheless it was in his power to throw it, for the moving force was in himself. Thus it is originally possible for the unjust and the intemperate not to become so, and they are therefore willingly such. But having become thus it is no longer possible to be otherwise. Indeed, not only are the evils of the soul voluntary but in some cases also those of the body, and we are blamed for these. No one reproaches those who are ugly by nature, but they reproach those who become so through lack of exercise and neglect. Similarly in respect to weakness and infirmity. For no one would blame a man who is blind by nature, or disease, or accident, but rather would they commiserate him. But all would blame him to whom this happened because of excess, or other forms of intemperance. Those physical ills, then, for which we are responsible are treated as a matter of blame, not those for which we are not responsible. If this is so, in the other cases also those evils which are subject to blame depend on ourselves.

Now if someone object that all people aim at the apparent good, and that they are not masters of their impression, but whatever form this takes, for each such does the end appear to him, (we reply that)—If each is in a sense the cause of his character, he will also be in a sense cause of the

form in which the good appears. If, on the other hand, no one
is the cause of his own evil doing, but each does these things
through ignorance of the end, because he supposes that
through this means he will effect the best, then the pursuit
of the end is not self-chosen, but one must have by nature, as
it were, a vision with which to discern well, and choose the
good in truth. Then he is indeed well-born who has this
noble endowment, for his will be the greatest and most
precious possession, which it is not possible to take or learn
from another, but such as one is by nature, such is the vision
one has. And to be well and nobly endowed by nature in this
respect would be the perfect and true form of good birth.
Now if this argument is true, in what respect would virtue
be more voluntary than vice? For to both alike, the good
man and the bad, the end appears and is fixed by nature, or
in whatever other way it comes, and with regard to the rest
it is with reference to this that they do whatever they do.
Whether, then, the end whatever it be does not appear to each
by nature, but is partly due to himself, or the end is indeed
by nature, and inasmuch as the good man voluntarily chooses
the means, virtue is voluntary, none the less would vice also
be voluntary. For there would equally in the case of the
bad man be something of himself in his actions, if not in the
end. If, therefore, as is maintained, the virtues are voluntary
—for we are in some sense part causes of our characters
and through being of such a character we set before ourselves such and such an end—so also are the vices voluntary.
For the same applies to them

Justice

Treated in Book V. of Aristotle's *Ethics*, now thought to be, as
also VI. and VII., actually the work of Eudemus, a follower of
Aristotle.
The passages illustrate the distinction emerging between the notion

of Justice as the complete fulfilment of Law, and the rational ideal
of Justice as aiming at Equality, in some sense.

Equity, a higher form of Justice, in some respects takes the place
of "Mercy."

THE NICOMACHEAN ETHICS V. i.

Let us take first the different senses in which a man is
called unjust.

It is held that the law-breaker is unjust, and the man who
grasps more than his share, and he who is unfair, so that it
is clear that the just will be the law-abiding and equal man.
Justice, then, is that which is according to law, and is equal;
injustice, what is lawless and unequal. Since, then, the unjust
takes more than his share, his business is not with goods of
all sorts, but those which belong to good and evil fortune.
These things are always good in an abstract sense, but not
always so for the individual. Yet men pray for them and pursue them. This they ought not to do, but to pray that what
is absolutely good should be good for themselves and to choose
the latter. . . . Again, it was said that the lawless man
is unjust; the law-abiding just. It is evident that in a
certain sense everything that is lawful is just. . . . And the
laws pronounce upon all matters aiming either at what is
for the common interest, or for the interest of the best people,
or those who are in power, or superior in some other way.
Hence from one point of view we call just, those conditions
which produce and preserve for the commonwealth the
elements of well-being, and well-being itself. And the law
enjoins also performance of acts of courage, such as not
abandoning one's post, or taking to flight, or casting away
one's arms; and of temperance, as abstinence from un-
chastity and outrage; and of gentleness, as not to strike, or
bring accusations. And similarly with the other virtues and
vices, commanding some, forbidding others, rightly where
it is rightly laid down, less well when carelessly drafted.
Thus understood, justice would be perfect virtue, not

absolutely, but in relation to others. Hence it is often thought
to be the greatest of the virtues, and neither the evening nor
the morning star so admirable, and as we say proverbially:
" In justice is present all virtue summed up." And it is
above all perfect virtue because it is the practice of perfect
virtue. Perfect it is because he who has it is able to exercise
virtue not only in himself, but also towards others. For
there are many who can be virtuous in matters relating to
themselves, but are incapable of it in their relations with
others. On this account does the saying of Bian seem good,
that office shows the man. For the holder of office is *ipso facto*
in relation to others and member of a community.

· · · · · ·

The Just Character

THE NICOMACHEAN ETHICS V. viii.

Just and unjust deeds being such as have been described,
a man is unjust or just whenever he acts in these ways
voluntarily. When involuntarily, he is neither unjust nor
just except accidentally, in so far as he effects results which
happen to be just or unjust. But the act of injustice or justice
is defined by the character of voluntariness or involuntariness. For when it is voluntary the person is blamed, and then
it is an act of injustice. Thus there may be an unjust act
which is not yet wrong, if the condition of voluntariness be
not added. And by voluntary I mean, as earlier said, whatever a man does knowingly of things which lie in his
own power.

· · · · · ·

It is a wrong when he acts with knowledge, but without
deliberation. . . . But when he acts with deliberate purpose, he is an unjust and vicious man.

Equity as a Finer Form of Justice

THE NICOMACHEAN ETHICS V. x.

In what follows I shall discuss Equity and the Equitable man; what is the relation of equity to justice, and of the equitable to the just. For on investigation they neither seem in all respects the same, nor different in kind. And sometimes we praise equity and the equitable man in such a way that we transfer the term, or use it instead of the term good, in praising people for all other qualities, besides showing that the more equitable is the more virtuous. Again, if we follow out the logical meaning, it seems strange that the equitable should be something praiseworthy beyond the just. For either the just is not good, or the equitable not just, if they are different, or if both are good, they are the same. Now the difficulty in regard to the equitable arises mainly on this account. These two are in every way right and in nothing contrary to each other. For equity is just, in the sense that it is a better form of justice and not better in the sense that it is something different in kind. For the just and the equitable are the same, and whilst both are good, the equitable is better. The source of the difficulty is that though equity is indeed justice, it is not justice of law but rather correction of a just law, and the cause is that every law is general, whilst there are cases in which a general rule cannot give a just decision. Where, then, it is necessary to lay down universal rules, and not possible to do so in all cases justly, the law assumes the general case, aware that there may be error. And it is none the less just. For the error is neither in the law, nor the legislator, but in the nature of things. For the material of practice is just of this kind. Whenever, then, the law pronounced is general, and a case occurs which is an exception, then it is right, where the legislator has overlooked the case, and erred because the pronouncement was general, to remedy the omission, as the legislator himself would also do were he present, and if he had known he would have legislated accordingly. Wherefore equity is just and better than the just in certain cases, not the absolutely just, but that which fails through lack of qualification. This is the reason why there are not laws for all circumstances, because there are some cases for which it is impossible to legislate, and a special decree is required. For the rule for what is indefinite must itself be indefinite, like the leaden rule in the Lesbian building. The rule is not fixed but adapts itself to the shape of the stone, and so does the decree according to that of the case. The nature of equity, and that it is justice, and in what sense better than justice, is thus clear. And it is evident from this what is the nature of the equitable man. For he is equitable who purposes to act in this way, and carries out his intention, not being extreme to mark what is done amiss, but willing to take less than his due although he have the law on his side. And this disposition is equity, being justice and not a distinct character.

．　　　．　　　．　　　．　　　．　　　．

In a passage on *Equity* in Aristotle's more popular treatise on *Rhetoric* (quoted by J. A. Stewart in *Notes on the Nicomachean Ethics of Aristotle*), he says further:

"And it is equitable to have sympathy with our fellow-men, and not to look to the law but the law-giver, and not to consider the word but the mind of the law-giver, nor the act so much as the purpose, and to regard not the part, but the whole. Again, not to examine what a man is now, but what he is always or generally, and to be mindful rather of the good one has enjoyed, than the evil, and the benefits one has received rather than those one has conferred. And to endure when wronged, and to prefer to be judged rather by deeds than words, as also to resort to arbitration rather than a law-suit. For the arbitrator considers what is equitable; the judge what is legal."

Practical Reason or Wisdom of Life

THE NICOMACHEAN ETHICS VI. v. To the "intellectual virtue" which Aristotle treats as especially concerned with practice, he gives a name which baffles translation, "Phronesis." It seems often to be nearer in meaning to "Wisdom of Life" than to "Practical Reason" (the usual translation). It is the outcome of an experience of unswerving following of the best course, and choice of the right so far as discerned, together with the constant intellectual effort to discover this ideal. A power of insight develops, a gift for unerring intuition both of principles and of the moral response required in every detail of a line of action. Mind and will are in perfect harmony in the character which possesses "Phronesis." It is a point of view, an attitude, a spirit, rather than a system of rules.

The difference between the most characteristic standpoint of Greek and modern Ethics could not be better expressed in a few words than by comparing Aristotle's dictum, "If wisdom of life be present, all the virtues are present," with that of Kant, "Nothing can be conceived either in the world or beyond it, which is absolutely good, except the good will."

The man of practical reason would appear to be one who deliberates well about matters which are good and beneficial to himself, not in a single sphere, as that of health or strength, but in relation to life as a whole. This is evident from the fact that we speak of people as having practical wisdom in some respect, when they reason well with a view to some worthy end where technique has no place. Thus the man of practical reason would be in general one who deliberates. Now no one deliberates about that which is inevitable, nor about what is not in his own power.

.   .   .   .   .   .

Practical reason can then only be a practical habit of insight into the truth in the field of human good and evil. In the case of artistic production the end is something beyond, but it is not so in the case of practice. For excellence in practice is itself the end. On this account we consider Pericles and men of that type to have practical wisdom, because they can discern what is good for themselves and good for mankind.

.   .   .   .   .   .

The principles of practice constitute the final end of action. But the man who is corrupted by pleasure and pain has no clear vision of the end, nor of the principle that one ought in all cases to choose and act for the sake of this, and with a view to it, for vice is destructive of the principle. Thus practical reason must be a formed habit guided by true reason, practical in the sphere of human goods. But whilst there are degrees of excellence in the sphere of art, there are no degrees of excellence in practical wisdom. And in the case of art it is preferable to err voluntarily, but in the sphere of practical reason, as with virtue generally, it is worse. Clearly, then, wisdom is a kind of virtue, and not an art. Now as the rational elements in the soul are two, practical wisdom is the virtue of that part to which opinion belongs. For opinion has to do with what is contingent, and so also practical wisdom. But it is not merely an intellectual state, as is evident from the fact that while such states admit of forgetfulness, practical wisdom does not.

.   .   .   .   .   .

vii.

Practical reason (or wisdom of life) is not only concerned with principles; it is also necessary to have insight into matters of detail. For it is practical, and practice has to do with particular things. Hence some who lack knowledge are more practical than others who have the knowledge, and amongst these, those who have experience.

.   .   .   .   .   .

xi.

(Light is thrown on the nature of this faculty by a survey of certain other faculties implied in it.)

That which we call considerateness, and in virtue of which we speak of people as sympathetic and having sensibility, is the right judgment of the equitable man. For it is the man of equity whom more especially we call sympathetic, and it is equitable to have sympathy in certain circumstances. And true sympathy is a discerning and just judgment of the equitable.

.   .   .   .   .   .

Equitableness is a common characteristic of all goodness in relation to others. All matters of practical life are concerned with particulars and ultimate facts, for the man of practical insight ought to know these, and discernment and considerate judgment have to do with practical facts, and these are ultimate.

.   .   .   .   .   .

xii.

There is a faculty which we call cleverness.

The nature of this is ability to perform the acts which further the aim set before us, and thus to hit upon the means. If, then, the end be noble, it is praiseworthy; if ignoble, cunning. Hence both men of practical reason and men who have cunning get the name clever. Now practical reason is not this faculty, but does not exist without it. The formed state of character, belonging to this eye of the soul, only develops with virtue.

.   .   .   .   .   .

The end and the best are not apparent, except to the good man, for vice turns us round, so that we lie in regard to practical principles. Evidently, then, it is impossible for any but the good man to have wisdom of life.

xiii.

(Natural virtue, or the endowment of good dispositions, is not virtue in the essential sense. Reason must be added, if these dispositions are to shine in action. Thus again wisdom of life is necessary to true virtue.)

Hence some say that all the virtues are forms of wisdom,

and Socrates was partly right in his enquiry; in part he erred. He erred in supposing that all the virtues were forms of wisdom; in thinking that they were inseparable from wisdom, he said well.

.   .   .   .   .   .

But whilst he held the virtues to be forms of reason (for they were all forms of knowledge), the way in which we put it is that they are accompanied by reason. It is obvious from what has been said that it is not possible to be distinguished in goodness without the wisdom of life, nor to have this wisdom without moral virtue. And in this way a solution would be found for the contention according to which it is argued that the virtues are independent of each other. For the same person is not well-endowed in respect to all, so that he may have already acquired one and not yet another. Now this is possible in the case of the natural virtues, but in respect to those in regard to which a man is said to be good in an absolute sense, it is not possible. For if wisdom of life alone be present, all the virtues are present.

.   .   .   .   .   .

Friendship

As suggested in the Introduction, the place of Friendship in Aristotle's system illuminates, and is illuminated by, a whole phase of Greek thought and life. It is part of the ideal of the valuable life, as already brilliantly expressed in Homer and in the drama, where it takes the two chief forms of the love of comrades, and of children of the same parents, or more particularly, sister and brother. In Plato it is the intellectual and spiritual bond of fellow-workers in the pursuit of truth which is the ideal form of friendship. In these books of Aristotle, friendship is especially studied as the greatest hope for political harmony. It is also conceived philosophically as representing in human society the principle of unity in the universe, and socially in the wide sense of the spirit of amity in all its forms.

THE NICOMACHEAN ETHICS VIII. i.

Next in order would follow the consideration of friendship; for it is a virtue, or accompanied by virtue, and moreover it is most necessary for life. For without friends no one would choose to live, though he had all other good things. Indeed the need of friends would seem greatest for the wealthy and those who hold offices and power. For what is the use of this kind of good fortune, if one is deprived of the opportunity of doing good, which is exercised most especially, and in its most praiseworthy form, towards friends? Or how would one be cared for and preserved without friends? For the greater the possession, the more it is exposed to danger. In poverty, moreover, and other misfortune, friends are regarded as the only place of refuge. By friendship the young are saved from error; the elder tended and aided in the actions they cannot complete through weakness. To those who have strength, it is a help to noble deeds—" when two advance together "—for they are more capable, both in thought and in act. It seems to be implanted by nature in the feelings of the parent for the offspring, and the offspring for the parent, not only in men but also in birds, and the greater number of animals, and in members of the same species towards each other; most of all amongst men; wherefore we praise those who love mankind. It may be noticed in travelling, how close akin and friendly is man to man. Friendship seems moreover to hold cities together, and legislators are more zealous about it than about justice; for unanimity, at which above all they aim, seems to be like friendship, and faction which is enmity, as far as possible they drive out. Nay when men are friends, they have no need for justice, but if just they still need friendship as well, and the height of justice appears to be of the nature of friendship. Not only is it a necessity—friendship is also a precious thing. We commend those who are lovers of friends, and to be rich in friendship seems to be a glory, and some think that the term friend is convertible with that of good man.

iii.

(There are three kinds of friendship, according as the motive and object are profit, pleasure or virtue. The two former are accidental, and easily dissolved, for if use or pleasure no longer attend the friendship, its occasion is gone.)

.   .   .   .   .   .

Perfect friendship is that of good men who resemble each other in virtue; for these, as good themselves, are equal in their desire of good things for one another, and they who desire good things for their friends, love them especially for the sake of these things. For they value them for what they are and not for something accidental. The friendship, therefore, of these men endures as long as they are good, for virtue is something stable. And each of them is good in himself and also in relation to his friend, for good men are both good absolutely and useful to each other. And they are equally sources of pleasure, both pleasant in themselves, and to each other; for to each his own actions and those similar to them are pleasurable, the activities of good men being the same or similar to their own. Now this kind of friendship ought to be lasting, since it combines in itself everything which should be characteristic of friendship; for every friendship is for the sake of good or pleasure, either absolutely or in relation to the friend, and in respect to some similarity.

.   .   .   .   .   .

Naturally it is rare, for there are few people of this kind. Moreover, it needs time and intimacy; for as the proverb says, it is not possible to know one another until people have consumed together the prescribed amount of salt; nor can they be satisfied that they are true friends, before each appear to each lovable and trustworthy. Those who are in haste to create marks of friendship with each other, desire indeed to be friends, but are not; unless they are worthy of

friendship and know it. The wish for friendship is swift
to arise but not friendship.

viii.

The majority on account of their love of honour seem
to desire rather to be loved than to love. Hence their
love of flattery; for the flatterer is, or affects to be, excessive
in friendship, and to love rather than be loved. And to be
the object of love seems near to being the object of honour,
at which the majority aim above everything else. . . .
But friendship seems to consist in loving, more than in being
loved. This is seen in the case of mothers, who delight in
loving; for some mothers give their children to others to
be reared, and continue to love them, since they know them,
but do not seek their love in return, if both are not possible.
Enough for them if they see their children prospering; they
love even though the children, on account of ignorance,
render none of those services which are seemly towards a
mother. Since, then, friendship lies more in loving, and it is
lovers of love who are praised, the virtue of friends seems
to consist in loving, so that those are constant friends who have
the gift for loving worthily, and theirs is the friendship
which endures. In this way more than any other even
those who are unequal can be friends, for thus they become
equal. Friendship lies in equality and likeness, and above all,
likeness in virtue; for being steadfast themselves, they are
constant with others, and neither ask of them aught that is
base, nor co-operate in such things. Nay, rather do they
hinder them; for it is characteristic of the good neither to
do wrong themselves nor to suffer this in their friends.

ix.

It seems, as we observed at the beginning of this discussion,
that friendship and justice have the same sphere; for there

appears to be some element of justice in every association, and so also of friendship. Fellow-voyagers and comrades in arms address each other as friends, and similarly the members of other associations. And in so far as there is community, so far is the friendship and also justice. And the proverb, " To friends all things are common," is true, for friendship lies in community. With brothers and comrades all things are common; with others, certain things are set apart, sometimes more, sometimes less, for there are degrees in matters of friendship, as also in matters of justice.

> .   .   .   .   .   .

Justice naturally increases together with friendship, for they exist in the same subjects, and are co-extensive in their application. Now all associations seem to form part of the political association; for people combine for the sake of some interest, and in order to secure the things that are good for life. And the political association seems both to have come together at the beginning and to endure for the sake of the common welfare; for it is this at which the legislators aim, declaring that justice is the common good.

IX. viii.

(Aristotle discusses the question of self-love. Ought we to love ourselves most or others? He observes that the love of self which is condemned means grasping too much of the things generally coveted. But this is not true self-love.)

(5)

If any man be zealous above all to act with justice or temperance, or generally in accordance with virtue, ever claiming as his own the nobler part, no one would call this man lover of self or condemn him. And yet such an one would be a self-lover in a truer sense; for he apportions to himself what is most valuable and good in the highest respect, and gratifies the most essential part of himself, and in all things is obedient to this. And even as a city and every other confederation seems to consist especially in the ruling part of itself, so also a man. And he is above all a self-lover who loves and gives pleasure to this element in his nature. Moreover, we speak of self-rule and self-misrule according as the mind has rule or not, as though this were the self. And those actions are thought to be done voluntarily which are essentially done with reason. It cannot then be doubted that, strictly, it is this which is the self and that the upright man cherishes this most. He, therefore, would be a true self-lover in a sense different from that in which self-love is disapproved, as far indeed from this as is the life in accordance with reason from that of passion, and the desire for the ideal from that for a seeming advantage. Now everybody approves and praises those who are in real earnest about noble deeds. And when all are rivals in virtue, and straining to do the noblest, duty would be common to all, and each have as his individual possession the greatest of goods, if virtue is such. In this sense the good man, since he will delight himself in the performance of noble acts and will benefit others, ought to be a self-lover, but not the bad man; for he will be hurtful to himself and his neighbours, following his unworthy passions. In his case there is a discord between what he does and what he ought to do, whilst what the upright man ought to do, that he does. For reason always chooses the best and the upright man obeys reason. Truly for righteousness' sake, and for his friends, he will do much, and for his country, if need be, he will die. Money and honours, and in general the goods for which people contend, he will freely give up, claiming for himself the ideal. To have this high pleasure for a short time he would choose in preference to a long period of indolence, and to live nobly for a year he would prefer to many years of ordinary life, and one noble and great deed to many petty doings. And this is perhaps the experience of those who die for others, for they choose for themselves a great prize. Such men will surrender money, so that their friends may receive more; thus the friend has money and the upright man the ideal good, and so the good he allots to himself is the greater. In like manner with honours and offices, all these he will give up to his friend; for this is a thing lovely for himself, and of good report. Surely he is thought to be worthy preferring the ideal before all things. It may happen that he gives up the deeds themselves to his friend, for it is the nobler part to become the cause of his friend's deed, than to do it himself. In this way the good man seems to apportion to himself the greater share of the best in all things praiseworthy. Thus it is right for him to be a self-lover in the sense defined, though not as the multitude understand the term.

ix.

The question may be raised whether the man who has true well-being will need friends or not; for it is said the happy and self-sufficing natures will have no need of friends, the things that are truly good being theirs. Since they are self-sufficient they do not lack anything, and the part of a friend as one's other self, is to obtain for his friend those things which he cannot procure for himself. Whence the saying: "When the soul is at peace what need of friends?" And yet it seems strange when ascribing all goods to the happy man, to deny him friendship, which is thought to be the greatest of external goods. And if it is more characteristic of a friend to be active in well-doing than passive; and if well-doing and virtue befit the good man, and there is something finer in the service rendered to friends than to strangers, the good man will have need of friends to serve. For this reason people enquire whether there is more need of friends in prosperity or in adversity, taking it for granted that the unfortunate has need of those who will succour him, and the fortunate of those whom they can benefit. Perhaps, indeed, it would be strange to make the happy man a solitary, for no one would choose the possession of every good thing in loneliness; for man is a social being, and fitted by nature to live with his fellows. And this is the case with the man who has true happiness; for he has the things which are naturally good, and it is evident that it is better for him to spend his time with friends and good men than with strangers and any chance acquaintance. Friends, then, are necessary to the happy man.

EPICURUS

342–270 B.C.

Epistle to Menoecius

Epicurus was an Athenian citizen born at Samos. In 310 B.C. he was teaching philosophy at Mitylene, but from 306 B.C. till his death he lived and taught at Athens. He appears to have led a truly philosophic life of simplicity, and wrote three hundred treatises. Although these are all lost (unless, as has been suggested, they may yet be found in the buried world of Herculaneum), a good deal is known about his doctrines, on account of the veneration for his teaching:

> "Epicurus who quenches all other lights as the celestia l sun rising puts out the stars."—LUCRETIUS.

Greek Text: Usener (from Diogenes), *Epicurea*.

In this epistle, which is believed to be genuine, Epicurus presents the essence of his moral philosophy. Philosophy is here understood as a spirit which leads to a certain kind of life. It will be evident that Epicurus' ideal for the wise man is in some respects far from that of later Hedonism. It is not upon the intensity of pleasures that he dwells, but upon the unruffled and untroubled mind in the healthy body. Epicurus' language here does not support Cicero's view that he meant by pleasure fundamentally physical pleasure. His portrait of the wise man has traits which remind us of Stoicism, but they lack the Stoic note of heroism.

Neither in youth put off the time for philosophy, nor in old age grow weary of philosophy; for it is never too early and never too late for attention to the health of the soul. He who says that the hour for philosophy has not yet come, or that it has gone by, is as one who should say that the hour for happiness has not yet arrived, or is no longer for him. Thus one ought to be a philosopher both in youth and in age; the latter that one may grow young again through contact with the good and remembering the past; the former so that one may be, even in youth, tranquil as the old in face of the future. We should then exercise ourselves in those

things which create happiness, since when this is present
we have everything; when this is absent, we do everything
to secure it.

The principles which I have never ceased to urge upon
thee, these both act upon and meditate, believing them to
be the elements of the good life. In the first place conceive of God as a living being, in-
corruptible and blessed, conforming in this to the universal
notion of God. Never attribute to God aught that is inconsistent with His immortality, or with His blessedness, but
think of Him as possessing everything which is capable of
contributing to His blessedness together with immortality.
For there are gods, and we have an unmistakable appre-
hension of their existence. But they are not such as the
majority suppose them to be. And it is not he who denies
the gods of the multitude who is impious, but he who
attributes to the gods what the opinions of the multitude
attribute. For the statements of the many concerning the
gods are not anticipations but false conceptions; as a result
of which the gods are the source of the greatest evils for bad
men, whilst from true conceptions come the greatest benefits
to the good. But the multitude, incapable of conceiving the
essence of virtue, except as that which is so regarded in their
experience, only accept gods conformable to this ideal, and
regard as absurd everything that is otherwise.

Accustom thyself to the thought that death is nothing in
relation to us; for good and evil consist in our perception
of them, and death is the deprivation of all perception.
Hence the right understanding of this truth that death is
nothing to us makes us capable of enjoying this mortal life,
not in setting before ourselves the prospect of an endless
time, but in taking away from us the longing for immortality. For there is nothing terrible in life for him who
has truly grasped that there is nothing in the beyond life.

Therefore he is foolish who says that death should be feared, not because it will be painful when it comes, but because it is painful to look forward to; for it is vain to be grieved in anticipation of that which distresses us not when present. Thus that which is the most awful of evils, death, is nothing to us, since when we exist there is no death, and when there is death we no more exist. Death, then, is neither for the living nor for the dead, since it does not exist for the former, and the latter are no more. But the multitude now flee death as the greatest of evils, now call for it as the cessation of the evils of life. The wise man neither pleads for life nor fears not to live; for neither is life a burden for him, nor does he suppose it an evil not to live. For as with food, it is not always the greatest quantity that we choose but the most dainty; so with time, it is not the greatest length which is enjoyed, but that which is fullest of pleasure. He, then, who appeals to the young to live well, to the old to end life well, is foolish, not only because the old have not yet taken leave of life, but because the discipline of living well and dying well is one and the same. Much more is he (Theognis) in error who says, " Best is it not to be born, but being born, as swiftly as possible to pass through the gates of Hades." If he says this with conviction, wherefore does he not depart from life? For this is always within his reach, if he desire it with resolution. But if he speak in jest, it was foolish so to address those who will not receive his words.

127.

With regard to the future, we ought to remember that it is neither wholly in our power, nor altogether beyond our power, so that we should neither await it as certain to come, nor despair of it as though assuredly not to be. We should consider in respect to our desires that some are natural, others are vain; and that amongst those that are natural, some are necessary, others only natural. Of those that are necessary, some are necessary for happiness; some for the tranquillity of the body; some for life itself. A sound theory of the desires should know how to relate all choice and avoidance to the health of the body and peace of the soul, since this is the end of the blessed life; for all that we do has this as its aim, that we shall neither suffer pain, nor trouble of mind. Once this has come to be, the whole tempest of the soul ceases, the animal being having no more cause to wander as in need of something, nor to seek anything else with which to complete the good of the body and the soul; for it is when we suffer from the lack of pleasure that we are in need of it, and when we are not in pain, we no longer need pleasure. It is for this reason that we say that pleasure is the beginning and the end of the happy life; for we recognise this as the first and native good, and this it is which gives birth to all choice and all avoidance. And, again, it is to pleasure that we come back, judging all that is good by the standard of feeling. And for the very reason that this is the first and natural good, we do not choose to take every pleasure, but there are occasions when we pass by many pleasures because greater distress follows upon them. Many pains, again, we value more than pleasures, because a greater pleasure will follow, if we endure the pains for long. Every pleasure, then, in its own nature is a good, but not every pleasure is desirable, even as all pain is evil, but not every pain is in its nature such as to be avoided. It behoves us, however, to judge all these things, weighing their consequences and examination of advantages and disadvantages; for there are times when we treat the good as evil, and the evil in turn as good.

Independence we hold to be a great good, not in the sense that we should always live on small resources, but so that if we have not much, we should be satisfied with little, being well assured that it is those who are least in need of abundance who derive from it the greatest enjoyment; that all that is natural is easily procurable; and that which is difficult to procure is valueless.

.   .   .   .   .   .

131.

When, therefore, we say that pleasure is the end of life, we do not speak of the pleasures of the abandoned and of those which consist in indulgence, as those suppose who are ignorant of our doctrine or disagree with it or misunderstand it, but we mean by pleasure the absence of suffering in the body and trouble in the soul. For it is not continuous drinking and carousals, nor the enjoyments of children and women, nor the taste of fish and other dishes of a lavish table, which produce the happy life, but a sober reason, capable of finding in all circumstances grounds for choice and avoidance, and the way of escape from those opinions through which the greatest confusion takes possession of the soul.

The principle of all this and the greatest good is wisdom. Therefore, wisdom of life is more honourable than philosophy itself. This is the natural source of all the other virtues, since it teaches that it is not possible to live agreeably without living prudently, well, and uprightly; nor to live prudently, well, and uprightly without pleasure. Thus the virtues of necessity grow together with the happy life, and the happy life is inseparable from them.

133.

Is there, then, any man whom thou canst consider superior to the sage, holding as he does the right views concerning the gods, and ever without fear of death, understanding also what is the end of Nature, comprehending that the cup of good things is easily filled; whilst evil is brief either in time or in grievousness? He can laugh at that fate which is averred by some to be lord of all. Rather, he says, that some events come through fate or necessity, some through fortune, and some lie with us. And whilst responsibility is not compatible with necessity, and fortune is obviously unsteady, that which lies in our own power, free from all alien dominance, is that to which blame and praise are rightly attached. And certainly it is better to follow the myths concerning the gods than to be enslaved to the fate of the physical philosophers. For the former brings hope of moving the gods by entreaty through honours rendered to them, whilst fate is inflexible in its necessity. The sage does not hold fortune to be a god as the multitude suppose, for nothing that is without order is done by God, nor does he hold it a cause seeing that it is uncertain. Neither does he believe that good or evil are bestowed on men by fortune for the happiness of life, but that the occasions of great good and evil are provided by fortune. Better he deems it to be unfortunate after wise reflection than to be lucky without reflection. The best thing, however, in action is to have right judgment, and on this account to succeed.

Meditate, then, upon these principles day and night, both by thyself and in company with one who is like-minded, and never whether waking or dreaming wilt thou be confounded in soul. And thou wilt live as a god among men. For he who dwells amid unperishable goods is in nothing like a mortal man.

Maxims of Epicurus

The following are taken from the Teubner Edition of the inscriptions discovered on the walls of the market-place of Oenoanda in Asia Minor in 1884, by the French scholar Holleaux, and consisting to a great extent of thoughts of Epicurus.

They were already known—from many references in Epicurean writings—and where the maxims are identical in Usener (*Epicurea*) references to Usener are given.

The arrangement in the Teubner Edition, by Johannes Williams, is indicated in the Roman numbering.

XLII.

The being which is blessed and immortal neither has any trouble itself, nor causes trouble to another. Hence it is affected neither by feelings of anger nor of favour, for all these feelings belong to weakness.

XLIII. (USENER 139).

Death is nothing to us, for that which has suffered dissolution has no sensation, and that which has no sensation is nothing to us.

XLIV. (USENER 139).

No pleasure is in itself evil. But those things which are productive of certain pleasures bring annoyances many times greater than the pleasures.

XLV. (USENER 141).

If those things which are productive of the pleasures of the abandoned released the mind from fears in regard to astronomical phenomena, and death, and pain, and taught how to limit the desires and pains, we should never have had any cause to complain of such persons, since they would in every way fill up the cup of pleasure, and would have been ignorant of pain and suffering—that is of evil.

LIV. (USENER 142).

It is not possible to live pleasantly without living wisely, nobly and justly; nor to live wisely, nobly and justly without living pleasantly. If in any man one of these is lacking (that is, living wisely, nobly and justly), it is not possible for him to live agreeably.

LVI. (USENER 140).

There is naught which is so capable of producing contentment as not attempting many tasks, nor undertaking harassing business, nor forcing oneself beyond one's capacity, for all these produce confusion in the mind.

LVII.

The all-essential in happiness is the state of mind, and

this is in our own control. To go to war is toilsome, though it be to rule others; the rhetorician's lot is full of violent emotion, even if he be capable of persuasion. Why, then, should we pursue these troublesome avocations, which it is open to others to undertake?

.   .   .   .   .   .

The following are taken only from Usener, *Epicurea*.

XII. (USENER 143).

It was not possible that the mind should be set free from terror in matters of greatest moment, whilst lacking understanding of the nature of the All, and possessed of suspicions in connection with myths. Thus it was not possible to enjoy unalloyed pleasures without the study of Nature.

XV. (USENER 144).

The wealth of Nature both has its defined limits and is easy to procure; that of vain opinions recedes to an infinite distance.

XVII.

The just man is freest from disturbance of mind; the unjust filled with the greatest confusion.

XIX. (USENER 145).

The pleasure of infinite time is equal to that which finite time possesses, if you measure its bounds by reason.

XXVII. (USENER 148).

Amongst the things which wisdom procures for the happiness of the whole of life, much the greatest is the possession of friendship.

Justice

XXXI. (USENER 150).

Natural Justice is a covenant for advantage neither to injure one another, nor to be injured.

XXXII.

Amongst those of the animals which are incapable of making contracts neither to injure nor be injured, there is neither justice nor injustice. Even so with peoples, who are either unable or unwilling to make contracts neither to do nor suffer wrong.

XXXIII.

Justice, then, is nothing in itself, but a certain mutual agreement arising in society—neither to wrong nor be wronged.

THE STOICS

The First Heads of the Stoa

Zeno, 336–264 b.c.; Cleanthes, 333–232 b.c.; Chrysippus, d. 208 b.c.

Zeno came from Citium, in Cyprus, and is said to have been partly of Phoenician descent. He came to Athens in 314, and after twenty years' study, founded the school at the Stoa (colonnade or porch) Poecile. Cleanthes, who succeeded him in the headship of the school, gave to the system a more Pantheistic character. Of Chrysippus of Soli in Cilicia, the third leader, it was said, "Had there been no Chrysippus there had been no Stoa." He appears to have given the doctrine its final form, and was a voluminous writer. But all the writings of the early Stoics have been lost, except the *Hymn to Zeus*, by Cleanthes. We have to depend on "fragments" collected by modern scholars from classical literature, or accounts of the system compiled by later writers.

The passages selected are translated mainly from the material collected in *Stoicorum Veterum Fragmenta*, by J. Von Arnim, a few from *Historia Philosophiae Graecae*, H. Ritter and L. Preller. I have thought it best to give Von Arnim's references to his sources, without the exact reference to the *loci*, as readers would probably consult Von Arnim first. Where not otherwise stated, the extracts are all from *Stoicorum Veterum Fragmenta* (volume and number of fragment given).

The World, the Soul, and Fate

ii. 300.

In their view there are two principles of all things—the active and the passive. The passive is the inactive substance, matter; the active the reason in it—God; for this, which is eternal in all substance, is the creator of individual things.

580.

And God is one, both Mind and Destiny, and Zeus, and also known by many other names. . . . The world is organised in accordance with reason and providence; mind extending through every part of it, even as with us, the soul. Thus the whole cosmos is a living being, ensouled and rational, having the ether as its ruling part, according to Antipater. But Chrysippus and Poseidon say that the heavens are the ruling part; Cleanthes the sun.—

DIOGENES LAERTIUS.

The Stoics declare that God is intelligence—a creative fire—moving to the production of the world, containing all the seed-giving laws of generation, by means of which all particular things come to be according to destiny.—PLACITA.

303d.

Our Stoics say, as you know, that there are two principles in the nature of things, from which all things become— cause and matter. Matter lies inert, having prepared the things for all developments, and would cease to be if no one endowed it with motion. But the cause, namely reason, gives form to matter, and turns it in whatever way it decides, and out of it produces the diversity of works. There must, then, be something out of which all comes, and again, that by which it becomes. The latter is the cause; the former, matter.—SENECA, *Epistle* 65.

In the opinion of Zeno, Cleanthes and Chrysippus, substance takes different forms as fire, and as seed, and again out of this brings to completion the constitution of things as before.—DIOGENES and STOBAEUS.

785.

If the Soul is a substance, it is either fire, or breath, composed of small particles extending through all the living body. If so, they obviously mean that neither is it the principle, nor is it any chance thing. For neither as wholly fire nor as wholly breath or wind has it this power. It would thus have a special form and reason and power, and as they say, *tension.*—ALEXANDER APHRODISIUS.

809.

The soul, in their view, is generated and destructible, not destroyed straightway on leaving the body, but enduring a certain space of time, by itself; the soul of the good until the destruction of all things by fire; that of the foolish, for a certain period of time.—ARIUS DIDYMUS.

811.

Cleanthes says that all souls endure until the conflagration; Chrysippus those of the wise only.

913.

According to Chrysippus, Destiny is the reason of the world, reason of those things that are ordained in the cosmos by Providence; reason according to which that which has been has come to pass, that which is, comes to be, that which will be, will come to pass. Again, for reason he substituted truth, cause, nature, necessity, and other names assigned to the sam   ng, according to the different occasions.—

STOBAEUS.

929.

The mind of God, that is Destiny, is incapable of deflection. For the Stoics called Destiny the Mind of God.—PROCLUS.

934.

But one soul extended through all, accomplishes all, each as part moved in the way in which the whole directs.—

PLOTINUS.

937 (extract).

It is not possible that anything in the parts, even the least, can happen otherwise than in conformity with the common nature, and in accordance with the reason belonging to it.—

PLUTARCH.

Fate and Free-will

984.

If it is said that those things are in our power, the contrary of which we are capable of doing, and it is in relation

to such acts that praise and blame are accorded, and exhortations and dissuasions, as well as punishments and
rewards, it will no longer be true that people are wise and
virtuous when possessing virtue, because no longer are
they capable of the vices contrary to the virtues. And similarly with the vices in the case of bad men, for neither is it
in their power no longer to be bad. But it would be strange
indeed, not to hold that the virtues and the vices lie in our
power, nor that praise and blame arise in respect to these,
since this kind of thing does not rest with us.—

ALEXANDER APHRODISIUS.

Chrysippus, however, both rejected necessity, and also
did not allow that anything happened without previous
causes. But he distinguished the kinds of cause, so as both
to avoid necessity and to retain fate. For amongst causes,
he said, some are perfect and primary; others contributory
and secondary. On this account, when we say that all things
happen by fate through antecedent causes, we do not wish
it to be understood that this is by the perfect and fundamental
causes, but by contributory and proximate causes. And if
these were not in our power, it would not follow that desire
is not in our power. For it can easily be explained, as he
thinks, in what sense judgments of assent are said to come
about through previous causes; for although assent cannot
be, unless moved by an object perceived, yet that object
is the immediate, not the principal cause. Thus it has the
explanation, as Chrysippus holds, which we gave a little
while ago, not that the occurrence indeed can take place
without the stimulus of an external force (for it is necessary
that assent should be influenced by the thing perceived),
but he refers to the cylinder and its revolution, which cannot
begin without being impelled. Nevertheless, when this
happens, he thinks that it is by its own nature which remains

over and above, both that the cylinder turns and the revolution takes place.—

CICERO, "DE FATO" (from *Ritter and Preller*, 411).

Evil

R.P. 403.

The world is a perfect body, but the parts of the world are not perfect, because their nature is such in relation to the whole and not in themselves.—PLUTARCH, *De Stoicis*.

Nothing is more foolish than those who think that good could have been, if there were not at the same time evil. For since good things are contrary to evil, each is necessary in opposition to the other, and as it were sustained by a reciprocal and hostile pressure to endure; for nothing is so completely contrary without the other contrary.—

GELLIUS on *Chrysippus*.

From *Von Arnim*.

Some there are who deem there is one only principle to offer as consolation, "That evil has no existence," as Cleanthes holds.

.   .   .   .   .   .

Cleanthes, indeed, consoles the wise man who does not need consolation; for nothing which is not base is evil. If you persuade the mourner of this, you cure him, not of his grief, but of his folly.—CICERO.

ETHICS

The End

I. 179.

Zeno was the first to say in his work on the nature of man that the end is to live in harmony with nature; that is, in accordance with virtue; for nature leads us to this.—

DIOGENES LAERTIUS.

Zeno declared the end to be to live in a state of conformity; this is to live in accordance with one harmonious principle, inasmuch as those who live in discord have souls ill at ease. Those who followed him, filling up the conception in detail, stated it thus: " To live in conformity with nature," thinking Zeno's saying to be a less complete proposition; for Cleanthes, his first successor as head of the school, added: " in accordance with nature," and thus rendered it: " The end is to live in conformity with nature." Chrysippus, wishing to make the principle clearer, introduced the following form: " To live in accordance with experience of those things which are in harmony with nature."—STOBAEUS.

III. 4.

It is the same thing to live according to virtue, and to live in accordance with experience of that which is in harmony with nature, as says Chrysippus in his first work on Ends; for our natures are part of the nature of the whole. Wherefore the end is to live in the following of nature. And this signifies in accordance with one's own nature, and in accordance with the nature of the whole, doing none of those things which the universal reason forbids; that is the right reason moving through all, the same for God, who ordains the government for all things. This is the virtue of the happy man and the even flow of life when all things are done in accordance with the harmony of the spirit of each individual in relation to the purpose of the governor.—
DIOGENES LAERTIUS.

16.

The end they say to be happiness, or that on account of which all things are done, whilst it is itself not done for the sake of anything beyond. And this consists in living according to virtue, in living harmoniously; again, what is the same thing, in life according to nature. Happiness Zeno defines in this way: Happiness is a calmly flowing life. Cleanthes also used this definition in his writings, and Chrysippus, and all their followers, saying that happiness is not different from the happy life. Happiness, however, they said lies at the end, the end being to aim at happiness, which is the same thing as to be happy. It is evident from this that to live according to nature has the same meaning as living nobly and living well; and again, to be an upright gentleman and possess virtue, and that all that is good is noble, and all that is base despicable. Hence the Stoic end is equivalent to the life of virtue.—STOBAEUS.

54.

Not only do they say this, but also beyond this, that the addition of time does not increase what is good, but even if there were for him but a moment of time, the wise man would lack nothing in respect to happiness, in comparison with one who practises virtue for a lifetime, passing his life blessedly in virtue.—PLUTARCH.

54.

Wherefore they say that in every respect and always, good men are happy, and the bad unhappy; and the happiness of the former differs in no way from the divine happiness, nor its character as indivisible, according to Chrysippus; and that the happiness of God is in nothing preferable, nor more beautiful, nor more sublime than that of wise men.—

STOBAEUS.

55.

Chrysippus declares in all his books on nature and morals that vice is a state of unhappiness, writing and insisting that to live according to vice is the same thing as to live miserably.—

PLUTARCH.

Good and Evil

I. 190.

Of existing things (as Zeno says) some are good, some evil, some indifferent. Examples of the good are wisdom, temperance, justice, courage, and all that is virtue or shares in virtue. Of evil, folly, incontinence, injustice, cowardice, and all that is evil, and shares in evil. Indifferent are life, death, fame, disrepute, pain, pleasure, riches, poverty, sickness, health, and what resembles these.

.   .   .   .   .   .

117.

They say (*i.e.*, Chrysippus and others) that, as it is a property of warmth to warm, not to make cold, so of the good to benefit, not to harm. But wealth neither benefits more than it injures; and so with health. Neither riches nor health, then, is a good. Again, they say, that thing which it is possible to use both well and ill, is not a good. Now it is possible to use both riches and health well and ill. Riches and health are not, then, goods, but things indifferent.—

DIOGENES LAERTIUS.

All these in common (Zeno, Chrysippus and others) laid down that virtue was a certain condition of the ruling element of the soul, and a capacity produced by reason. Or more especially, they said that it was a kind of reason, harmonious, steady, and unchangeable. And they do not hold the emotional and irrational part to be distinguished by a certain difference of nature from the rational part of the soul, but that the same element which they call understanding and the ruling part turning through the whole and changing in its states (these changes being in relation to habit or condition), becomes both vice and virtue, and that there is no irrational part in it. But it is called irrational, whenever through powerful excess of impulsion getting the upper hand it is carried towards some abnormal end, contrary to the choice of reason. For this state is evil and intemperate, reason acquiring violence and strength from bad and mistaken judgment.—PLUTARCH.

Of the Wise and the Unwise

I. 216.

Zeno and the Stoic philosophers who follow him hold that there are two classes of men, and that the class of the good practise virtue through the whole of life; the class of the bad, vice. Hence those of the former kind are always upright in everything with which they have to do, whilst those of the latter go wrong. And the good man using the experiences of life does everything well in his actions, and with wisdom, and temperance, and the other virtues; the bad man does the opposite, evil in all.—STOBAEUS.

No Degrees in Sin

224.

They hold that all forms of wrong-doing are equal, as Zeno says.—DIOGENES LAERTIUS.

Tension

The conception of tension (*tonos*) appears, though a product of Greek thought, to be peculiar to the Stoics. In the Universe it is the force which spiritualises matter, sometimes regarded as fire. Applied to ethics it seems to be the perfect harmony of the spirit whose strength is exactly proportioned to its work, straining after the best, yet in full control of its energy, harmoniously poised like the athlete of the statue, whose power is shown in symmetry and restraint.

I. 563.

Cleanthes in his *Physical Commentaries* says that tension is like a flash of fire, and that if it is sufficient in the soul to accomplish all that falls to it, it is called strength and force. This strength and force when it is displayed in endurance, where steadfastness is required, is self-control; when undergoing dangers, courage; when in matters where value is in question, justice; in cases of choice and giving way, temperance.—PLUTARCH.

And just as strength of the body is a sufficient tension in the nerves, so strength of the soul is a sufficient tension in regard to judging and doing, or not doing.—STOBAEUS.

On Right and Law

III. 308.

Justice is by nature and not by institution, as also law and right reason, as Chrysippus says in his work on the Whole.—

DIOGENES LAERTIUS.

314.

Chrysippus thus began in his book on Law: Law is King of all, gods, and human affairs. And it ought to be the determining principle of what is noble and base, and the ruler and leader, and accordingly the standard in respect to just and unjust, and amongst those animals which are by nature political, that which determines what should be done, and forbids what should not be done.

326.

Hear what they say concerning these things in the third work on the Gods:

"It is not possible to find any beginning of justice, nor origin, except from God and the common nature." For thence should everything of this kind have its commencement, if we are to say anything concerning good and evil.—

PLUTARCH.

327.

The Stoics say that heaven is rightly their city—on earth there are no cities; the city they say does not exist. For the city is a good thing and a whole of parts well-fitted together, and the multitude of men organised under law.—CLEMENS.

EPICTETUS

ABOUT A.D. 50 TO A.D. 130

A slave, freed after the death of Nero, A.D. 68. Expelled from Rome with other philosophers by Domitian, A.D. 89, he went to Nicopolis, and lectured there till his death. His addresses were recorded by Arrian, who heard him. He is almost unknown except from his writings, which show him, as Mr. P. E. Matheson says (from Bonhöffer) in the Introduction to his translation of Epictetus' *Discourses and Manual*, to be a Stoic of the old school.

Chapter 1. Text: *Epicteti Dissertationes*, Heinrich Schenkl; *Enchiridion* (Manual), J. Schweighaeuser (Teubner). Translation: P. E. Matheson.

MANUAL

Of all existing things, some are in our power, and others are not in our power. In our power are thought, impulse, will to get and will to avoid, and, in a word, everything which is our own doing. Things not in our power include the body, property, reputation, office, and, in a word, everything which is not our own doing. Things in our power are by nature free, unhindered, untrammelled; things not in our power are weak, servile, subject to hindrance, dependent on others. Remember, then, that if you imagine that what is naturally slavish is free, and what is naturally another's is your own, you will be hampered, you will mourn, you will be put to confusion, you will blame gods and men; but if you think that only your own belongs to you, and that what is another's is indeed another's, no one will ever put compulsion or hindrance on you; you will blame none, you will accuse none, you will do nothing against your will; no one will harm you, you will have no enemy, for no harm can touch you.

209

Aiming, then, at these high matters, you must remember that to attain them requires more than ordinary effort; you will have to give up some things entirely; and put off others for the moment. And if you would have these also—office and wealth—it may be that you will fail to get them, just because your desire is set on the former, and you will certainly fail to attain those things which alone bring freedom and happiness.

.   .   .   .   .   .

Chapter 5.

What disturbs men's minds is not events, but their judgments on events. For instance, death is nothing dreadful, or else Socrates would have thought it so. No, the only dreadful thing about it is men's judgment that it is dreadful. And so when we are hindered, or disturbed, or distressed, let us never lay the blame on others, but on ourselves—that is on our own judgments. To accuse others for one's own misfortunes is a sign of want of education; to accuse oneself shows that one's education has begun; to accuse neither oneself nor others, shows that one's education is complete.

.   .   .   .   .   .

Chapter 11.

Never say of anything, "I lost it," but say, "I gave it back." Has your child died? It was given back. Has your wife died? She was given back. Has your estate been taken from you? Was not this also given back? But you say, "He who took it from me is wicked." What does it matter to you through whom the Giver asked it back? As long as He gives it you, take care of it, but not as your own; treat it as passers-by treat an inn.

.   .   .   .   .   .

Book I., chapter i.

But what says Zeus? "Epictetus, if it were possible I would have made your body and your possessions (those trifles that you prize) free and untrammelled. But as things are—never forget this—this body is not yours, it is but a clever mixture of clay. But since I could not make it free, I gave you a portion in our divinity, this faculty of impulse to act and not to act, of will to get and will to avoid; in a word, the faculty which can turn impressions to right use. If you pay heed to this, and put your affairs in its keeping, you will never suffer let nor hindrance; you will not groan, you will blame no man, you will flatter none. What then? Does all this seem but little to you? Heaven forbid!"

. . . . . .

But, as things are, though we have it in our power to pay heed to one thing and to devote ourselves to one, yet, instead of this, we prefer to pay heed to many things and to be bound fast to many—our body, our property, brother and friend, child and slave. Inasmuch, then, as we are bound fast to many things, we are burdened by them and dragged down.

Citizenship of the Universe
Chapter viii.

If these statements of the philosophers are true, that God and men are akin, there is but one course open to men, to do as Socrates did, never to reply to one who asks his country, "I am an Athenian," or "I am a Corinthian," but "I am a citizen of the universe." For why do you say that you are an Athenian, instead of merely a native of the little spot on which your bit of a body was cast forth at birth? Plainly you call yourself Athenian or Corinthian after that more sovereign region which includes not only the very spot where you were born, and all your household, but also, generally, that region from which the race of your forbears has come down to you. When a man, therefore, has learnt to understand the government of the universe and has realised that there is nothing so great or sovereign or all-inclusive as this frame of things wherein men and God are united, and that from it comes the seed from which are sprung, not only my own father or grandfather, but all things that are begotten and that grow upon earth, and rational creatures in particular —for these alone are by nature fitted to share in the society of God, being connected with Him by the bond of reason —why should he not call himself a citizen of the universe and a son of God? Why should he fear anything that can happen to him among men? When kinship with Caesar or any other of those who are powerful in Rome is sufficient to make men live in security, above all scorn and free from every fear, shall not the fact that we have God as maker and father and kinsman relieve us from pains and fears?

Attitude to the Wrong-Doer

Chapter xviii.

They are thieves and robbers.

What do you mean by thieves and robbers?

They are gone astray and know not what is good and what is evil.

Ought we then to be angry with them or to pity them? Only show them their error and you will see how they desist from their faults. But if their eyes are not opened, they regard nothing as superior to their own judgment.

What! you say, " Ought not this robber and this wrong-doer to be put to death? "

Nay, say not so, but rather, " Should I not destroy this

man who is in error and delusion about the greatest matters, and is blinded not merely in the vision which distinguishes white and black, but in the judgment which distinguishes good and evil?" If you put it this way, you will recognise how inhuman your words are; that it is like saying, " Should I not kill this blind man, or this deaf one?" For if the greatest harm that can befall one is the loss of what is greatest, and a right will is the greatest thing in everyone, is it not enough for him to lose this, without incurring your anger besides? Man, if you must needs harbour unnatural feelings at the misfortune of another, pity him rather than hate him; give up this spirit of offence and hatred; do not use these phrases which the backbiting multitude use, " These accursed and pestilent fools."

On the Will

Chapter xxix.

The essence of good and of evil lies in an attitude of the will.

What are external things, then?

They are materials for the will, in dealing with which it will find its own good or evil.

How will it find its good?

If it does not value overmuch the things that it deals with. For its judgments on matters presented to it, if they be right, make the will good, and if crooked and perverse, make it bad. This law God has ordained and says, "If you want anything good, get it from yourself."

Life, a Soldier's Service

Book III., chapter xxiv.

Do you not know that life is a soldier's service? One man must keep guard, another go out to reconnoitre, another

take the field. It is not possible for all to stay where they
are, nor is it better so. But you neglect to fulfil the orders
of the general, and complain when some severe order is
laid upon you; you do not understand to what a pitiful state
you are bringing the army so far as in you lies; you do not
see that if all follow your example, there will be no one to
dig a trench, or raise a palisade, no one to keep night-watch
or fight in the field, but everyone will seem an unserviceable
soldier.

The Part and the Whole

Book IV., chapter vii.

Can reason and demonstration teach no one that God
has made all things in the world, and the world itself as a
whole to have its own end without hindrance, but its individual parts to subserve the whole? Now all other things
are without the capacity of understanding His governance,
but the rational creature has faculties that enable him to
reflect on all these things, to realise that he is a part, and what
part he is, and that it is well for the parts to give way to the
whole. And, further, being by nature noble and generous and
free, he sees that he has some of the things about him unhindered and in his own control, and some again subject
to hindrance and dependent on others, the acts of his will
unhindered, and things beyond his will subject to hindrance.
And, therefore, if he makes up his mind that his good and his
interest lie in the former alone, in things that are unhindered,
and depend upon himself, he will be free, tranquil, happy,
unharmed, high-minded, reverent, giving thanks for everything to God, on no occasion blaming or accusing anyone
for what happens.

.   .   .   .   .   .

Fragment from Epictetus on Friendship

Which of us does not admire that saying of Lycurgus the Lacedaemonian? For when one of his young fellow-citizens had blinded him in one eye and was handed over to Lycurgus by the people to be punished as he chose, he did not punish him, but educated him, and made a good man of him, and brought him before the Lacedaemonians in the theatre, and when they wondered, he said, "This man, when you gave him me, was insolent and violent; I give him back to you a free and reasonable citizen."—

Flor. XIX. 13.

These lines are ascribed to Cleanthes:

Lead me, O Zeus, and lead me, Destiny,
Whither ordained is by your decree.
I'll follow, doubting not, or if with will
Recreant I falter, I shall follow still.

P. E. MATHESON.

R

THE THOUGHTS OF
MARCUS AURELIUS ANTONINUS

Born A.D. 121.   Emperor A.D. 161.   Died A.D. 180

He was engaged in wars during a great part of his reign. To the fact that Stoicism was a philosophy for practical men, there is no better witness than these thoughts of the student called to the uncongenial life of the Emperor of the Roman world in this stormy period. Much of his journal appears to have been written in the countries on the Danube where the war was going on.

Greek Text: *D. Imperatoris Marci Antonini, Commentariorum quos sibi ipsi scripsit Libri XII. Recensuit,* Johannes Stich (Teubner). Translation by George Long.

II.

1. Begin the morning by saying to thyself, I shall meet with the busybody, the ungrateful, arrogant, deceitful, envious, unsocial. All these things happen to them by reason of their ignorance of what is good and evil. But I, who have seen the nature of the good, that it is beautiful, and of the bad, that it is ugly, and the nature of him who does wrong, that it is akin to me, not only of the same blood or seed, but that it participates in the same intelligence and the same portion of the divinity, I can neither be injured by any of them, for no one can fix on me what is ugly, nor can I be angry with my kinsman, nor hate him. For we are made for co-operation, like feet, like hands, like eyelids, like the rows of the upper and lower teeth. To act against one another, then, is contrary to nature; and it is acting against one another to be vexed and to turn away.

2. Since it is possible that thou mayest depart from life this very moment, regulate every act and thought accordingly. But to go away from among men, if there are gods, is not

a thing to be afraid of, for the gods will not involve thee in evil; but if, indeed, they do not exist, or if they have no concern about human affairs, what is it to me to live in a universe devoid of gods or devoid of providence? But in truth they do exist, and they do care for human things, and they have put all the means in man's power to enable him not to fall into real evils. And as to the rest, if there was anything evil, they would have provided for this also, that it should be altogether in a man's power not to fall into it. Now that which does not make a man worse, how can it make a man's life worse? But neither through ignorance, nor having the knowledge, but not the power to guard against or correct these things, is it possible that the nature of the universe has overlooked them; nor is it possible that it has made so great a mistake, either through want of power or want of skill, that good and evil should happen indiscriminately to the good and the bad. But death certainly, and life, honour and dishonour, pain and pleasure, all these things equally happen to good men and bad, being things which make us neither better nor worse. Therefore they are neither good nor evil.

. . . . . .

IV.

4. If our intellectual part is common, the reason also, in respect of which we are rational beings, is common; if this is so, common also is the reason which commands us what to do, and what not to do; if this is so, there is a common law also; if this is so, we are fellow-citizens; if this is so, we are members of some political community; if this is so, the world is in a manner a state. For of what other common political community will anyone say that the whole human race are members? And from thence, from this common

political community, comes also our very intellectual faculty and reasoning faculty and our capacity for law; or whence do they come? For as my earthly part is a portion given to me from certain earth, and that which is watery from another element, and that which is hot and fiery from some peculiar source (for nothing comes out of that which is nothing, as nothing also returns to non-existence), so also the intellectual part comes from some source.

.   .   .   .   .   .

23. Everything harmonises with me which is harmonious to thee, O Universe. Nothing for me is too early nor too late, which is in due time for thee. Everything is fruit to me which thy seasons bring, O Nature: from thee are all things, in thee are all things, to thee all things return. The poet says, " Dear city of Cecrops," and wilt not thou say, " Dear city of Zeus "?

.   .   .   .   .   .

27. Either it is a well-arranged universe, or a chaos huddled together, but still a universe. But can a certain order subsist in thee, and disorder in the All? And this, too, when all things are so separated and diffused and sympathetic?

.   .   .   .   .   .

V.

3. Judge every word and deed which are according to nature to be fit for thee; and be not diverted by the blame which follows from any people nor by their words, but if a thing is good to be done or said, do not consider it unworthy of thee. For those persons have their peculiar leading principle and follow their peculiar movement; which things do not thou regard, but go straight on, following thy own nature and the common nature; and the way of both is one.

.   .   .   .   .   .

18. Nothing happens to any man which he is not formed by nature to bear. The same things happen to another, and either because he does not see that they have happened, or because he would show a great spirit, he is firm and remains unharmed. It is a shame, then, that ignorance and conceit should be stronger than wisdom.

19. Things themselves touch not the soul, not in the least degree; nor have they admission to the soul, nor can they turn or move the soul; but the soul turns and moves itself alone, and whatever judgments it may think proper to make, such it makes for itself the things which present themselves to it.

.   .   .   .   .   .

21. Reverence that which is best in the universe; and this is that which makes use of all things and directs all things. And in like manner also reverence that which is best in thyself; and this is of the same kind as that. For in thyself also, that which makes use of everything else is this, and thy life is directed by this.

VII.

9. All things are implicated with one another, and the bond is holy; and there is hardly anything unconnected with any other thing. For things have been co-ordinated, and they combine to form the same universe. For there is one universe made up of all things, and one God who pervades all things, and one substance, and one law, one common reason in all intelligent animals, and one truth; if, indeed, there is also one perfection for all animals which are of the same stock and participate in the same reason.

.   .   .   .   .   .

22. It is peculiar to man to love even those who do wrong. And this happens, if when they do wrong it occurs to thee

that they are kinsmen, and that they do wrong through ignorance and unintentionally, and that soon both of you will die; and above all, that the wrong-doer has done thee no harm, for he has not made thy ruling faculty worse than it was before.

.   .   .   .   .   .

68. It is in thy power to live free from all compulsion in the greatest tranquillity of mind, even if all the world cry out against thee as much as they choose, and even if wild beasts tear in pieces the members of this kneaded matter which has grown around thee. For what hinders the mind in the midst of all this from maintaining itself in tranquillity and in a just judgment of all surrounding things, and in a ready use of the objects which are presented to it, so that the judgment may say to the thing which falls under its observation: "This thou art in substance (reality), though in men's opinion thou mayest appear to be of a different kind "; and the activity shall say to that which falls under the hand: " Thou art the thing that I was seeking; for to me that which presents itself is always a material for virtue both rational and political, and, in a word, for the exercise of art, which belongs to man or God." For everything which happens has a relationship either to God or man, and is neither new nor difficult to handle, but usual and apt matter to work on.

69. The perfection of moral character consists in this, in passing every day as the last, and in being neither violently excited nor torpid, nor playing the hypocrite.

.   .   .   .   .   .

X.

6. Whether the universe consists of atoms, or nature is a system, let this first be established, that I am a part of the whole which is governed by nature; next, I am in a manner intimately related to the parts which are of the same kind

with myself. For remembering this, inasmuch as I am a part, I shall be discontented with none of the things which are assigned to me out of the whole; for nothing is injurious to the part, if it is for the advantage of the whole. For the whole contains nothing which is not for its advantage; and all natures, indeed, have this common principle, but the nature of the universe has this principle besides, that it cannot be compelled even by any external cause to generate anything harmful to itself. By remembering, then, that I am a part of such a whole, I shall be content with everything that happens. And, inasmuch as I am in a manner intimately related to the parts which are of the same kind with myself, I shall do nothing unsocial, but I shall rather direct myself to the things which are of the same kind with myself, and I shall turn all my efforts to the common interest, and divert them from the contrary. Now, if these things are done so, life must flow on happily, just as thou mayst observe that the life of a citizen is happy who continues a course of action which is advantageous to his fellow-citizens, and is content with whatever the State may assign to him.

GEORGE LONG.

THE END

INDEX OF AUTHORS, WORKS, AND CHIEF ETHICAL SUBJECTS

DEMCO